"For academics and interested lay readers w... ...g ... ... they may enter the expansive theological scope of the educational enterprise, Shatzer provides a relentlessly accessible framework for thoughtful reflection. He balances an introductory overview of numerous intersections of faith and learning with a nuanced exploration of the disciplines that constitute the university curriculum. In the end, it is an encouraging word for thoughtful teaching and Christ-centered colleagueship."

—**Gene Fant,** *president, North Greenville University*

"Christian colleges and universities are filled with faculty who love the Lord, but who have never been challenged to think theologically about their academic work. Helping them bridge the gap between doctrine and their disciplines is one of the most important components of faculty development in Christ-centered institutions. In *Faithful Learning*, Jacob Shatzer provides us a great short introduction to theology, yet the application reflections by scholars in various fields make this the ideal book to help faculty wrestle with how Scripture applies to their teaching and research. We will be using *Faithful Learning* at our university for many years to come."

—**Nathan A. Finn,** *provost and dean of the University Faculty, North Greenville University*

"One of the great opportunities for faculty new to the Christian university is the time and expectation that they will think deeply about the intersections between their faith and scholarly work. Shatzer's *Faithful Learning* provides an excellent starting point. The concise theological introductions followed by examples from different disciplines will give these new faculty an excellent resource to begin this journey."

—**Nathan Lane,** *associate provost and dean of the Catherine T. MacArthur School, Palm Beach Atlantic University*

"I wish *Faithful Learning* had been around when I started my teaching career. Jacob Shatzer has penned a valuable primer for any faculty member just starting out in Christian higher education. Succinct yet comprehensive, *Faithful Learning* will indeed leave the reader hungry to know God more fully."

—**Barbara McMillin,** *president, Blue Mountain College*

"*Faithful Learning* is a great help to all in Christ-centered higher education. For a book that starts with *norma normans non normata*, it engages faculty in ways that no other systematic theology text does—and we are all the better for it. Grounded, theologically orthodox, and helpful as we think about living out our faith in various disciplines. It is also an encouragement for young scholars who want to use their intellectual gifts to the glory of God."

—**Samuel W. "Dub" Oliver,** *president, Union University*

Faithful Learning

Faithful Learning

A Vision for Theologically Integrated Education

Jacob Shatzer

foreword by David S. Dockery

ACADEMIC
BRENTWOOD, TENNESSEE

For Ben Mitchell and Dub Oliver

Contents

Foreword

Christian higher education involves a distinctive way of thinking about teaching, learning, scholarship, service, subject matter, student life, administration, and governance that is grounded in the orthodox Christian faith. In this new volume that you hold in your hands, Jacob Shatzer has provided readers with a clear understanding of the phrase, "grounded in the orthodox Christian faith." Moreover, he offers applicable ways for implementing a theologically shaped vision across the disciplines for faculty and staff who serve on the campuses of Christian colleges and universities, doing so through his conversation partners in each chapter representing these various disciplines. *Faithful Learning: A Vision for Theologically Integrated Education* provides us with insightful guidance for thinking about how and what we teach as well as how and what we learn. Most importantly, this brief and readable book enables us in practical and accessible ways to wisely consider what we believe, how we think, how we prepare students, and how we serve both church and society.

Encouraging all involved in Christian higher education to move beyond basic markers of Christian piety and Christian activism, as important as these things may be, Shatzer proposes a foundational theological vision to sustain the mission of Christian higher education. This volume recognizes that a failure to do so will result in ambiguity about the very meaning of Christian higher education. This third decade of the twenty-first century is a critical time for us to refocus on the meaning and mission of Christian higher education to discern the distinctive reason for its existence. In this secular age characterized by spiritual confusion, moral anarchy, polarization, and fragmentation, we need to revisit the core confessions of our faith.

The reality is that the terms "theology" or "Christian doctrine" scare many people who are associated with Christian colleges and universities. These terms, which are not necessarily synonymous but can be used interchangeably as we are doing here, sound formidable, abstract, and technical. Others even suggest that theology is irrelevant for our lives in general and our serious academic work in particular. While the suspicion of theology or Christian doctrine is not limited to those who serve in academic settings, it is nevertheless present there. Recognizing that theology is what the church believes, teaches, and confesses based on the Word of God, to borrow thoughts from the influential historical theologian Jaroslav Pelikan, we can begin to take a first step toward seeing how the study of theology provides what Kevin Vanhoozer has called an "anchored set" that informs all other academic disciplines in an interrelated way for the glory of God.

Building on the ideas of other important Christian thinkers, we can begin to think of theology as developing a mind for truth so that we can indeed articulate the faith once for all delivered to the saints (Jude 3) while shaping a heart for God so that our lives and academic communities are built up in the faith. Such an approach to theology will have Scripture as its foundation, Christ as its center, the church as its focus, and the influencing of society and culture as a key element of this work.

With Jacob Shatzer, we believe that Christian doctrine can render service to Christian higher education in multiple ways. It addresses the mind so that we can know the triune God as the revelation of himself to us. Theology also informs and undergirds the mission of Christian higher education, making it vital for teaching, for connecting the academy with the church, and for the task of cultural engagement. This new volume thus points us in a fresh way to understand what we believe as well as how our lives are to be lived and how our classes are to be taught. Such beliefs and practices come from serious theological reflection on the teachings of Scripture as well as the contributions of influential Christian thinkers throughout church history.

One of the goals of Christian higher education is to guide and enable our students as they seek to live in the world with a lifestyle that issues in glory to God. Shatzer helps us begin to connect the dots to see anew the implications of a theological vision for our shared work as Christian educators, refocusing questions related to how Scripture bears upon the various academic disciplines, how we reappropriate the best of the Christian intellectual tradition, how we clarify our confessional commitments, and how we engage the academy and the culture in this rapidly changing cultural context.

Certainly, such an endeavor is not without its challenges. We will need to begin with an acknowledgment that we will approach the education enterprise from the perspective of faith seeking understanding. Shatzer takes this first step without any attempt to ground the work in a particular denominational tradition but by seeking to develop a framework to cultivate a holistic orthodoxy based on a high view of Scripture, congruent with the Trinitarian and Christological consensus of the early church. *Faithful Learning* moves us toward an understanding of the importance of confessional convictions, informing both the core and boundaries of our work. Our author and his conversation partners winsomely articulate these foundational commitments by connecting Christian doctrines with the various academic disciplines.

This book is designed to enable faculty and those involved in faculty development programs to grasp the basic teachings of Christian theology to begin to think biblically, Christianly, and faithfully, bringing scripturally informed faith to bear upon every discipline, what some have called faithful learning. Following the apostle Paul, we want to emphasize the Christ-centered approach to such a proposal. In Eph 4:21, we are reminded that "you heard about him [Christ] and were taught by him, as the truth is in Jesus." In many ways, what needs to be recognized is that Jesus Christ is not only the subject matter in our educational pursuits, but he is also the teacher and the context in which the teaching takes place. Thus, ultimately Shatzer's proposal points readers to Jesus Christ, which with broader application will point colleges and universities toward a greater depth of understanding of what is involved in their Christ-centered identity and mission.

To think of Christ-centeredness only in terms of Christian experience, while important, will be inadequate. Shatzer's work envisions a faithful Christian higher education that exalts Christ in a way that is tightly tethered to the church's confessional tradition, which is necessary for the health and well-being of Christians and Christian academic institutions. The result of such efforts will help Christian faculty, staff, and students understand the God who has made himself known and to provide a Christian understanding of God's creation and redemptive work in the world.

While Shatzer is not proposing that all faculty members need to be academic theologians in the technical sense, he does call for those who serve in Christian higher education to recognize their responsibility to understand these foundational Christian teachings. He also wants Christian academics to grasp how these beliefs influence and shape their calling as scholars, teachers, and leaders in the academic world. No one should think that theology is the whole of academic life, but there must be a place for a holistic love of God, for Jesus has told us to love God with our heart, soul, strength, *and* mind, and to love our neighbor as well.

Shatzer's invitation in *Faithful Learning* is anything but a cold intellectual approach to the Christian faith unaccompanied by affection. This volume does not think of theology or Christian doctrine as a kind of intellectual aloofness or merely an intellectual curiosity lacking heartfelt commitments. Instead, we are given a holistic proposal to help educators reflect on the meaning of human nature, who we are in Christ, where we stand in the universe, how we think about teaching and learning, and the place of relationships in a community of people who have experienced the forgiveness of sins through the redemptive work of Jesus Christ and the indwelling presence of the Holy Spirit in our lives.

This important volume will encourage Christian faculty to move beyond an unhealthy individuality as well as beyond a suspicion of the theological enterprise. Moreover, this work, if implemented in faculty development programs for newer and seasoned faculty at Christian campuses across this country and in other parts around the globe, will begin to strengthen much-needed cross-fertilization between theologians and those who serve in other disciplines within the academy. This overarching theological vision will prayerfully pave the way to help us recover a renewed understanding of our calling to serve faithfully in Christ-centered institutions.

The theological vision represented in this volume can help those who are called to serve in Christian higher education to better understand what they believe and why they believe it. An appreciation of our theological heritage and the best of the Christian confessional tradition will help keep us from confusing what is merely a contemporary expression from that which is enduringly relevant. It will also encourage humility and a dependency on God's Spirit and the primary source of our theology in Holy Scripture. Christian scholars will be able to see their teaching and their scholarship as contributing to the unity of knowledge. Faculty and students will be able to work together to enhance a love for learning that encourages a life of worship and service.

I applaud Jacob Shatzer for putting together this delightful, insightful, and helpful volume. I believe that now is the right time to reconsider the importance of such a theological vision, especially when considering the challenges and disorder across the academic spectrum. The theological commitments called for and articulated by Shatzer provide the very backbone, the underpinnings of distinctive evangelical higher education. Beyond this, such a vision will seek to connect head, heart, and hands. Shatzer's work seeks to connect theology and ethics. To do otherwise will result in a generation of faculty and students who fail to take every thought captive to Jesus Christ (2 Cor 10:5). Faith and courage will be needed for these efforts. Moreover, we will all need wisdom to have our minds opened and ordered, trusting God for further guidance and illumination for our journey.

David S. Dockery
President, International Alliance for Christian Education

Introduction

While I do not remember off the top of my head the first book I purchased from Amazon—the online behemoth—Amazon, of course, does. I placed the order on December 9, 2002, and it included a book filled with authors who would change my life, not only through their writings, but later, through their teaching and investment in me. The book? *Shaping a Christian Worldview: The Foundations of Christian Higher Education.*[1] When I placed the order, I was a sixteen–year-old high-school senior, hoping to study at Union University. By the time I graduated from Union in 2007, I'd been taught by roughly half the contributors in courses ranging from art history to biblical studies, from advanced English grammar to philosophy, from William Faulkner to C. S. Lewis. My Christian worldview had definitely been shaped.

The seeds of this book were sown in that one, but not primarily because of books and writing. That book certainly impacted my thinking, and I hope that this book will influence yours. But that is not why I'm fondly recalling that first Amazon order. The people who wrote those chapters became my professors, with all the personal investment that goes along with that at a small, Christian, liberal arts–based university. I experienced the way they thought and taught, but I also saw how they lived, how they celebrated life's joys and mourned its sorrows. God has used some of them to show me profound examples of faithfulness over the years. But not all. For a few also introduced me to the pain of seeing teachers and mentors turn from their own best insights and admonitions. For all the shelter that Christian universities can provide in the name of focused learning, they are still filled with us, with people. And but for the grace of God, all things fall apart.

---

[1] David S. Dockery and Gregory Alan Thornbury, eds., *Shaping a Christian Worldview: The Foundations of Christian Higher Education* (Nashville: B&H Academic, 2002).

But why this book? For all the strengths and weaknesses of the Christian worldview conversation—and I do not intend to solve those debates here—Christians need to be able to think and talk about theology, and Christian academics need to be able to do so right along with our talk about our disciplines. And if we are honest, sometimes that is uncomfortable. While some faculty may have a rich background of theological knowledge, many struggle to get started. This book is meant to be a very basic entry point for those faculty, as well as a common text that can generate further conversations and explorations with faculty with a variety of previous exposures to theology. By growing in our abilities to think theologically, we not only grow in our own faith, we also better serve the students whom God has entrusted to us. In short, the point of this book is to equip faculty to be key instruments in faithfully transforming students in all disciplines.

A CHRISTIAN THEOLOGY OF LEARNING

There are three ongoing debates about Christian learning that help us to see how crucial—and difficult—this transformative approach is. First, the adequacy of "worldview thinking" has been under fire. Second, Christian scholars have explored how best to consider human beings as knowers, especially the relationship between the intellect and the affections. Finally, the very terminology of "integrating faith and learning" has its critics. While I will not seek to solve any of these debates here, their rough outlines will help us better see—and feel—the need for Christian academics across the disciplines to explore Christian doctrine.

Many Christian scholars have approached these issues through the lens of "worldview" and "worldview thinking." But some have critiqued the notion of worldview, arguing that it is far too intellect-dependent, or impractical, or forced. To some, "worldview thinking" implies that we can all hit pause on our lives, sort out our worldview issues in our minds, and then get back into things. To draw out the more lived—and often implicit—forms of life that inevitably shape the way humans know, some Christian teachers, such as David I. Smith, have drawn in the vocabulary of the "social imaginary." This term helps emphasize those implicit elements that worldview can miss; that much of our thinking is embedded in, shaped by, and related to ways of doing things that fly under the radar most of the time. This line of thinking emphasizes the role that practices play in our knowing.

Highlighting this debate sets us up to see more fully the way Christian doctrines interact with academic disciplines. "Worldview" has had a profound impact in helping Christian scholars work out how the truths of God connect with the truths discovered in our disciplines. Ideas such as the "social imaginary" encourage us to expand our thinking beyond, well, our thinking!

Christian education cannot simply focus on information and our minds but must focus on holistic human beings. In short, education is about more than head knowledge. While this sort of statement has never been absent from Christian education, some think that the emphasis on the head has deformed our approaches. Jamie Smith has brought this argument to the forefront in books such as *Desiring the Kingdom* and *You Are What You Love*. As he puts it, "What if education wasn't first and foremost about what we know, but about what we love?"[2] For, as humans, "Our wants and longings and desires are at the core of our identity, the wellspring from which our actions and behavior flow."[3] In other words, humans are complex beings, and while brains and information matter, we must address the whole person. There is certainly some pushback worth giving here; for instance, Smith himself makes his arguments primarily through books, which address the intellect more than the heart, and he may sometimes overemphasize wants and longings and desires, as the quote above. Plus, it is the *knowledge* of the gospel preached, to some degree, that the Holy Spirit uses to change radically our wants and longings and desires. I think it is fair to take the critique from Smith that education is about more than information, while also being cautious not to run entirely away from the central importance of Christian *thinking*.

Another debate surrounds the language of faith and learning itself. One of the most prominent ways of talking about these issues is "the integration of faith and learning." But that language itself is not without detractors, partly because of the various ways it can be used.[4] To some, the terminology itself

---

[2] James K. A. Smith, *Desiring the Kingdom: Worship, Worldview, and Cultural Formation* (Grand Rapids: Baker Academic, 2009), 18.
[3] James K. A. Smith, *You Are What You Love: The Spiritual Power of Habit* (Grand Rapids: Brazos, 2016), 2.
[4] For more on this, see Susan VanZanten, *Joining the Mission: A Guide for (Mainly) New College Faculty* (Grand Rapids: Eerdmans, 2011), 109.

makes the problem sound too normal, as though faith and learning have long gone about their business happily on their own. In reality, the Christian faith has not only been foundational in multiple fields of study, but even fields that claim secularity often demonstrate the qualities of faith—it's just not faith in the God of the Bible! Additionally, "integration of faith and learning" can make it sound like this integration is something that faculty must figure out how to achieve rather than something that is already there. As one of my colleagues, Phil Davignon, has helpfully put it: We don't make the integration happen. The integration is there, in Christ. We are just seeking to discover it.

Due to these challenges, some Christian scholars seek to move beyond using "worldview" and "integration." For instance, Susan VanZanten does not think the terms are recoverable and instead proposes to use the idea of "faithful learning."[5] While I agree that new terms and ideas might emerge that bring along the positives of worldview, faith integration, and holistic learning, I am also sure that any new phrases will come with their own limitations and detractors! Instead, we can carefully use these terms, recognizing and attempting to account for the limitations that others have found and that we ourselves might stumble over as we go along.

DOCTRINE AND THE DISCIPLINES

While every discipline can connect with a primary doctrinal area,[6] a basic understanding of a fuller scope of Christian doctrine positions faculty to do the kind of careful, faithful integration work that our students need. Put another way, every academic discipline can be related to one primary doctrinal connection. At the same time, the very nature of Christian doctrines, and the way that they connect with one another, means a broader understanding of Christian doctrine is needed as well.

There are multiple reasons for this need. First, Christian doctrines are not easily isolated from one another. So, for instance, if your discipline seems to relate most clearly to the doctrine of creation, your understanding of the doctrine of creation is bound up with a growing knowledge of the doctrine

---

[5] VanZanten, 121.
[6] For a helpful example of this, see the chapter "The Doctrines and the Disciplines" in Harry Lee Poe, *Christianity in the Academy: Teaching at the Intersection of Faith and Learning* (Grand Rapids: Baker, 2004), 115–32.

of God and the doctrine of eschatology. In my doctrine classes, I'm always inviting students to notice and explore these connections. The integration of faith and learning presses us into these connections too. We should not stop once we identify a primary doctrinal connection; we must press for deeper understanding.

Second, we need to be honest about a temptation in connecting our faith with our academic disciplines. As one scholar identified thirty-five years ago:

> Like children long rejected, evangelical scholars are still too anxious to be accepted by their peers, too willing to move only in directions that allow them to be "relevant." The result is that we have been far more inclined to speak up when our Christian convictions are in tune with the assumptions of modern academic life than when they are at odds. It is much easier, for instance, to set oneself in the vanguard of social progress than it is to defend those Christian assumptions that the established and fashionable intellectual circles of our day regard as obscurantist and fanciful. Yet it is this tougher mental fight that we must not avoid.[7]

In short, it is much easier to point out the places where our Christian faith connects to our disciplines and will be applauded by the broader academy or culture. But if we are honest and if we look, we will notice places where the Christian faith challenges the assumptions of our disciplines. We will not get applause there, and we are often tempted to downplay that in favor of the former. Part of faith integration means identifying these challenges and working creatively through them, not just avoiding them.

These realities impact the format we will follow in this book. To gain a broader understanding of Christian doctrine, each chapter will present one major Christian doctrine. I am a Baptist theologian, but my attempt is to explain what Christians agree on. Yet, I acknowledge that mine will always be a Baptist perspective (and, particularly, one thoroughly formed by the work of

---

[7] Nathan Hatch, "Evangelical Colleges and Christian Thinking," in *Making Higher Education Christian: The History and Mission of Evangelical Colleges in America*, ed. Joel Carpenter and Kenneth Shipps (Grand Rapids: Eerdmans, 1987), 166–67.

the great Baptist theologian Millard Erickson).[8] The point of this book is not to be the final word in your exploration of Christian doctrine, but a quick way to get a sense of the whole. I want you to explore your traditions more carefully, and I hope you leave each chapter with detailed questions that will press you into the Bible and into more specific books. Each chapter will conclude with some related Scripture and further reading suggestions.

There is one more important piece to each chapter, and these are my favorite parts. Each chapter also includes a contribution from a Christian scholar in a field other than Bible or theology. I asked these contributors to help me explore how the chapter's doctrine fit with their discipline, as well as how that doctrine confronts some of their disciplines' assumptions. I am also convinced that Christians in various academic disciplines see things about doctrinal truths that can help the church, so I asked each to reflect on whether there was something about the chapter's respective doctrine that his or her discipline sees a bit more clearly than people think. In other words, every discipline has something positive to contribute to the broader church's understanding of such doctrines. I am indebted to these faculty for their insights, and I am confident you will benefit from them.

CONCLUSION

As I mentioned earlier, my hope is that this book will help you grow in your faith and in your work in your own discipline. I pray it plays a small role in shaping you, and that you, in turn, will play a small role in God's work in the lives of your students. As valuable as books can be, and as valuable as I hope this one is, it is the careful and painstaking work of discipleship that we are called to in Christian higher education. Just as those authors in *Shaping a Christian Worldview* impacted me, my hope is that you will influence the students God has entrusted to your care.

---

[8] See Millard Erickson, *Christian Theology*, 3rd ed. (Grand Rapids: Baker, 2013) and L. Arnold Hustad, ed., *Introducing Christian Doctrine*, 3rd ed. (Grand Rapids: Baker, 2015).

1

Doing Theology

How do we talk about what we know about God? What do we listen to, or give authority to, when we try to understand God and the things of God? What do we do if the sources of authority seem to conflict?

You might think you are comfortable with your answer to this question. Perhaps you're used to saying, "The Bible is the ultimate authority." But what else do we draw on, and what do we do when we get conflicting signals?

Christians typically refer to four sources when we talk about authority and theology. The Wesleyan quadrilateral is the name that is given to these four sources of theology.[1] The four sources are *Scripture, reason, tradition*, and *experience*. Some use the metaphor of a four-legged stool, but that metaphor confuses us because it makes each of the legs seem very similar, both in structure and structural importance. It's almost implied that we give Scripture one vote, reason one vote, tradition one vote, and experience one vote. That's not exactly right. One question to keep in the back of your mind as we explore these various sources is, "How do these relate in my understanding of the truth about God?" Or perhaps even more interestingly, "How does the way my academic field defines what counts as 'knowledge' impact the way I think about knowing God?"

SCRIPTURE

When we think about Scripture as a source, the Reformation provided us with a helpful phrase: *norma normans non normata*. This Latin term basically means that the Bible is the norm, or standard, that norms—or standardizes—our knowledge of God without itself being normed or standardized. The standard

---

[1] Erickson, *Christian Theology*, 226 (see intro., n. 8).

that standardizes cannot be standardized. The *norma normans non normata*, in other words, is the authority that exercises control over all the other authorities, and itself never submits to those other authorities. Scripture regulates our reason. Scripture exercises authority over our views of tradition. And Scripture stands over, authorizes, and standardizes our experience of God.

A second way to consider the authority of Scripture and its relationship to other authorities comes by distinguishing two types of authority. Baptist theologian Millard Erickson is helpful here. He distinguishes between a legislative and a judicial authority.[2] A legislative authority makes laws, and a judicial authority interprets the laws. According to this division, Scripture is the only legislative authority. Reason, tradition, and experience, then, are judicial authorities, helping us interpret and understand the authority of the Bible. We can see the Scripture as the only legislative authority while acknowledging the role that experience, tradition, and reason play as authorities in the theological task.

Scripture is the supreme authority exercising these functions over theology because it is divine revelation. But why do we need revelation? Ultimately, the answer to that is related to what we believe about God. As we think about the need for revelation, it depends on the fact that if we are going to know something about God, it is not the same as simply knowing something about ourselves or knowing about the world around us. That's because the fundamental distinction in all that exists is that between created things and the Creator. We are created; God is Creator. We do not know things about the Creator in the same way that we know about created things. Only God can cross that divide and make himself known to us. By his grace he has. He has made himself known, and Christians refer to that as revelation. We need revelation because we are creatures. We need revelation simply because God is God, and we are not.

Consider the idea of transcendence. "Transcendent" carries that idea of being above or over. And when we talk about the transcendence of God, we are talking about the distinction between God and everything else; as the Creator, he is above and over all the things that he has created. The transcendence of God is the idea that the things of God are so high and so wonderful that

---

[2] Millard Erickson, *Introducing Christian Doctrine*, 3rd ed. ed. L. Arnold Hustad (Grand Rapids: Baker Academic, 2015), 74.

humans cannot know them fully, simply because we are not God. We need revelation because God is transcendent.

Because of God's grace, the truth does not stop at transcendence. God is not a God who remains far off. Instead, God chooses to draw near, to make himself known. This drawing-near is God's immanence. He is close to us. On the one hand, God is transcendent, over and above all that he has made. The most fundamental divide is the divide between God and all that God has made. But stopping there leaves us with something like the god of deism—a god who created the world but then left it alone. When you have both transcendence and immanence, it reminds us that not only is God over and above us, but God has chosen to communicate himself to us.

We see this on some level in how God created humans in his image, which we will explore more when we get to the doctrine of humanity. We also see it when we talk about Jesus, fully God and fully man, God drawing near. In Christ we have transcendence, and we have immanence. As far as revelation goes, however, we can simply note that we can know something about the transcendent, over-and-above God because he has graciously created us to know him by creating us in his image, and he has come down to make himself known. He is immanent, and this makes revelation possible.

Two general categories cover the ways that God makes himself known: general revelation and special revelation. General revelation is the way that God communicates to all people, in all places, and at all times, through the world that he has made. The Bible points to this with statements such as, "the heavens declare the glory of God" (Ps 19:1). We also see in the book of Romans that all people everywhere can see enough of God's revelation in the world around them to be accountable for believing (or not believing) that God exists (Rom 1:18–25).

If general revelation is how God has made himself known in creation, special revelation is how God has made himself known through his Word. This covers both the Word of God, the Bible, and the Word as a name for the Second Person of the Trinity, who took on flesh and lived among us (John 1:14). God is a God who has spoken, in his Word and in the Son.

Three terms help us to further understand the character of special revelation. First, the Bible is inspired. "Inspiration" means "breathed out by God," indicating that it has God as its source. This term stems from 2 Tim 3:16, in which Paul invents a term, "God-breathed," to characterize Scripture. When we talk about the inspiration of the Bible, this is what we mean: God is the cause of these words, even if in a mysterious way that included and did not override human writers as causes of these words as well. "Inspiration" is used in a variety of ways in our everyday speech, and we must note one here that is potentially confusing. When Christians say that the Bible is inspired, we do not mean that it is merely inspir*ing*. By the work of the Holy Spirit, it certainly often is inspiring! But to say the Bible is inspired does not refer to the effect it has on its readers, but the fact that it is a product of God.

This fact of inspiration leads to a second term, important though more controversial in some traditions. Many Christians today also find it important to talk about the Bible as inerrant. "Inerrant" means without error, but more specifically that the Bible is true in all that it affirms. Confusion abounds with this term simply because in the modern world our understanding of error is calibrated according to disciplines and standards that have only recently been discovered (historiography, biology, physics, and so on).

The Christian belief in inerrancy does not come out of an inductive investigation of every single one of the Bible's claims, as if we've been able to dig up the remains of every ancient settlement mentioned in the Old Testament or something. Rather, the doctrine of inerrancy is a result of deductive reasoning, working backwards from what we know to be true of God. God is a God of truth, without any mixture of error. If the Bible is the God-breathed Word of this God of truth, it too is truth, without any mixture of error. The doctrine of inerrancy is really about the doctrine of God.

Now, as I mentioned, this term is more controversial. Some Christians find it unhelpful because modern standards of evaluation are so precise. Others think that things such as grammatical irregularities must be errors. Both charges are misunderstandings of inerrancy. At its root, this doctrine is about the reliability and goodness of God, and his ability to choose to reveal himself truthfully even if not completely.

Our third term moves away from describing Scripture and instead reminds us something about the reality of being human, and that term is "illumination." The doctrine of illumination reminds us that because sin infects every aspect of our humanity, we need God's gracious work in us to read and understand what he has revealed in his Word and in his world. Through the powerful work of the Holy Spirit, God "illumines" or "shines light" on his Word, impressing it on our hearts and minds. We will explore this more when we talk about the impact of sin, but it is important to note here in thinking about how we go about *doing* theology that at every point we are reliant upon God's gracious work, in the world, in his Word, and in our hearts and minds.

General revelation and special revelation are both results of God's gracious choice to show himself to us. Revelation cannot conflict because God is One and is consistent. If we think something we see in the world related to God conflicts with Scripture, the mistake is ours. When some Christians play "Jesus" over against other portions of the Bible (whether those other portions be the Old Testament or the letters of Paul), the mistake lies at their feet. Thinking that revelation conflicts is a clear indication that we're missing something. We shouldn't deny our confusion, but we also shouldn't pretend that we have to pick one or the other. In fact, often when this is done, we pick something that we ourselves understand best or want most, and we try to force our understanding of revelation into that. If we truly rely on God to break through our limitations and confusions in order to reveal himself, we should be suspicious of ourselves when we force conclusions from our side. That is far more likely to be human manipulation than divine revelation.

TRADITION

The definition and role of tradition varies among Christians. Tradition, most simply, is "what has been handed down." It can include everything from official church teachings in some churches, such as the Roman Catholic Church, to statements of faith to the writings of important pastors and theologians from the past in other churches.

The difference extends to the authority that tradition carries. According to the *Catechism of the Catholic Church* (see part 1, section 1, chapter 2, article 2), tradition falls under the same type of God's work as Scripture itself. In other words, both Scripture and tradition are explained as an outflow of God's choice to reveal himself. They trace this back to a distinction between what the apostles wrote down (Scripture) and what the apostles handed down through their other teaching (tradition). This distinction continues through the official teaching ministry of the church. The key here is to realize that for Christians like these, the question is not putting tradition on the same level of Scripture but recognizing that both Scripture and tradition are part of the same gracious work of God. Protestants, however, simply disagree that tradition is best tied that closely to Scripture. This disagreement traces all the way back to the critique of the church that Martin Luther provided in his famous *95 Theses.*

While Protestants disagree with placing tradition on the same level of authority as Scripture, they don't toss tradition altogether. Even groups that rally to the cry of "No creed but the Bible" operate with some elements of tradition.

In their book *Who Needs Theology?*, Stanley Grenz and Roger Olson give four main Protestant distinctives on tradition.[3] First, Protestants reject tradition as equal with the Bible, so the idea that tradition and the Bible are the oral and written transmission of God's revelation is rejected. Protestants do not see tradition as equal with the Bible, but as interpretation and application of the Bible. Second, Protestants reject natural theology as a reliable guide on its own. In other words, to what degree can we just look at the world around us and understand God from it? Protestants reject this as a reliable guide because of the doctrine of sin, which has disrupted the way the world works and then also disrupts the way our minds work. Third, Protestants affirm the ability and right of every believer to read and interpret the Bible. In the Roman Catholic Church, there's a very important role that God gives the teaching ministry of the church, the magisterium, to aid in interpretation and understanding. Protestants don't reject the fact that there are some who are given unique insight and given roles of leadership and roles of teaching. However, this insight does not rise to the level of God's Word.

The downside to this third point is that people disagree on how to interpret the Bible, and sometimes these disagreements are harsh and divisive. Just look at the proliferation of Protestant denominations, based often on different interpretations of Scripture. Or just search a moment for an anecdote: surely you can think of a time at a Bible study or a Sunday school class or a university coffee shop conversation in which two people disagree on what the Bible says. Such realities can make a strong person—or a strong tradition—attractive. But for Protestants, the answer is not to exalt tradition to the same level of Scripture, because that can tend to exalt some Christians over others. This is related to a Baptist distinctive, the priesthood of all believers. All believers are called into a direct relationship with God through the merits of Christ. There is no

---

[3] Stanley J. Grenz and Roger E. Olson, *Who Needs Theology? An Invitation to the Study of God* (Downers Grove, IL: IVP Academic, 1996), 83–84.

priesthood, whether that is a priesthood for interpreting things or a priesthood for sacrificing things, or anything like that between the believer and God.

Grenz and Olson's fourth difference relates to who is supposed to *do* theological reflection. Theological reflection is an ongoing task of God's people. Protestants tend to emphasize that, more than simply reading the Bible, thinking about the Bible and endeavoring to understand God are vital pursuits for every believer. God's people must do these tasks together in community in the local church. But they are also the individual's responsibility.

How then does tradition benefit Christians, even if it is not on the same level of authority as the Bible? Grenz and Olson see the purpose of using the tool of tradition to connect us with the church of all ages as we seek to construct an orthodox Christian theology in the contemporary situation.[4] Another Baptist theologian, Millard Erickson, adds a few things that we've covered already:[5] Tradition provides insight into Scripture. It helps detect the essence of doctrines; in other words, as you read about the doctrine of Christ over the history of the church, you can get a sense of what are the most important pieces here that are agreed on. It also puts beliefs in cultural and historical perspective, and it helps us relate to other viewpoints more faithfully. There are a lot of good things that tradition as a source of theology can do when it's rightly ordered, when it's put in the right relationship with the other ways that God teaches us.[6]

REASON

Reason is central to the practice of theology. Scripture tells us that, in a sense, God is reason. He has ordered the universe according to plan. John 1 uses the idea of the underlying rationality of the universe to talk about Christ. Jesus is the *logos*, which carries with it his idea of rationality of the universe, structured in a certain way, according to a plan. We could define reason as a way of getting at and learning from God's general revelation, what he has revealed in the created world.

Reason is also central to the practice of theology because we will inevitably use reason as we think about and articulate our understanding of God. As one theologian puts it, we exercise reason when we do such things as analyze facts

---

[4] Grenz and Olson, *Who Needs Theology?*, 98.
[5] Erickson, *Introducing Christian Doctrine*, 8–10.
[6] Grenz and Olson, *Who Needs Theology?*, 98.

and ideas, construct arguments, form judgments, and decide what is true or false.[7] These actions assist us in the task of theology when we employ them to discern how Scripture holds together and what it requires of our lives. This use of reason often takes the form of drawing out implications from the teachings of the Bible.

At one level, we see reason as an important aspect of theology because reason helps us understand what we learn from other sources, and it also helps us to know how to apply and put into action some of those things. But we can think of reason in another sense as well. It is a source for our thinking about God when we talk about reason in the sense of thinking about the world that God has made. We do this across the university and different disciplines. Thinking about this in the context of a university is helpful. Academic disciplines are all seeking truth and seeking to know true things about the world. As Paul says in Romans 1, all humans can look around and see that God exists. Reason, according to Scripture, gets us that far at the very least.

EXPERIENCE

Finally, let us talk about experience. It is hard to handle experience well as a source for theology. On one hand, experience is necessary for theology. As Christians we worship a personal God who moves and speaks in history, in real life. Our human lives are full of experiences, good and bad, of the world, other creatures, and of God. Even our connection to the church brings with it a vast array of experiences. When we sit and read our Bibles on our own, there is still an experiential component. We simply do not have the option to ignore experience when doing theology, because of our nature as humans and because of God's existence as a personal God who has made himself known in the world of our experiences.

Luther approached the lived nature of theology directly. He wrote, "It is by living, indeed, by dying and by being damned, that one becomes a theologian, not merely by understanding, reading and speculation."[8] There is something about living life, experiencing life, experiencing life with God, feeling separated

---

[7] Beth Felker Jones, *Practicing Christian Doctrine: An Introduction to Thinking and Living Theologically* (Grand Rapids: Baker Academic, 2014), 23.

[8] Quoted in Timothy George, *Theology of the Reformers* (Nashville: B&H, 2013), 61. According to George, Luther repeated this basic idea several times throughout his works.

from God at times, that really teaches us about who God is. On one level, experience is a source simply because we are always experiencing, and God is working in the world and working in us.

In another way, experience can serve as a test for whether doctrines we believe fit with what we know is true about reality. Experience can be a good test. Does what we say we believe fit with reality? But this impulse to consider experience can lead to abuse, when we use something that we misunderstand (but think we do understand) about our experience to reimagine who God is. Let me give you a positive example of using experience and an example of abuse. First, we can see the truth of using experience as a test when we think about the doctrine of God. Some argue that if you just love God enough and pray enough, you will be rich beyond your wildest dreams. But that does not fit with experience, which then leads us back to reexamine what the Bible actually teaches. And it does not teach that.

But let us turn to consider an example where experience can be abused. Sometimes we are so confident in our understanding of the world, the broken world by the way, that we think we can dictate to God what can or cannot be true. This is a great temptation in our culture because we have seen great advances in human knowledge in so many different realms. We are used to figuring things out, and we develop high levels of certainty based on the methods we use. For instance, some might use the knowledge we have, through experimentation and experience, of human DNA to say that the doctrine of human sin must not be true, because we do not see anything about the fall encoded in our genes. We can become overly confident in our experience of the world and our interpretation of the world, and this overconfidence can lead us to turn around and tell God what he can or cannot say.

It's helpful to think of experience as a test of doctrine, but not the primary test. We must always be on our guard about our tendency to exalt our own thinking. We should defer to the Bible; the tie should go to the obvious teaching of Scripture whenever possible.

If you find yourself wanting to correct Scripture based on your experience, stop. Reconsider. It is an issue of proper ordering. We should not say that experience takes priority over the clear revelation of Scripture, but we also should not say that experience does not matter at all. God is living and active and moving today. We should be open and hopeful of God working in people's hearts. Just remember that God is consistent with who he says he is. The evidence of the Holy Spirit's work will never be different from what God reveals in the written Word.

METHOD

As we begin to consider theological method, the first question for us is simply, "How do these four sources of authority relate to one another?" As we reflect on how we think about and know things about God, does each source just get a vote?

Since we began with the idea of Scripture as the *norma normans non normata*, you should already sense that we can't go the route of one vote each. Instead, these sources provide different types of authority that work together in our theological method to develop our understanding of God. As biblical scholar N. T. Wright has put it, these sources "are not so much like apples, pears and oranges as like apples, elephants and screwdrivers. . . . Scripture is the bookshelf; tradition is the memory of what people in the house have read and understood (or perhaps misunderstood) from that shelf; and reason is the set of spectacles people wear in order to make sense of what they read," while experience deals with the effects of that reading.[9] You might recall our earlier distinction between legislative and judicial authority. The challenge of doing theology is not giving Scripture, tradition, reason, and experience each a vote. Rather, the challenge of doing theology is understanding what God has revealed in his Word, which intersects with these other ways we can see and experience the God of the Bible, who is personal, consistent, active, holy, and loving.

CONCLUSION

Discerning the relationship between various sources of authority is no easy task. One of the most basic questions that we must return to, however, is, "Am I truly submitting to the authority of Scripture, or am I using other authorities and reasons to weaken God's Word to me?" This is a question that we can never

---

[9]   Kevin J. Vanhoozer and Daniel J. Treier, *Theology and the Mirror of Scripture: A Mere Evangelical Account* (Downers Grove, IL: IVP Academic, 2015), 232–33; quoting N. T. Wright, *The Last Word: Scripture and the Authority of God—Getting Beyond the Bible Wars* (San Francisco: HarperOne, 2006), 101.

finally answer, but only continue to ask as we seek to understand what God has said and how we must respond.

———————

Naming the Unnameable: An English Perspective
AARON BROWN

Language is intimately connected with the nature and action of God. At the beginning of all things, the Creator *spoke* our world into existence (Gen 1:3). The first moment of the world as we know it came into existence with a line of pure poetry—"let there be light." It is hard to know how wonderful it must have sounded in the voice and language of God.

God then named the sky and the waters and called them good. From his very words, he expressed his desire to make human beings "in our image" (1:26). We see in Genesis 2 that part of Adam's calling on earth was to name the beasts of God's creation (Gen 2:19–20). The Genesis account is all about naming and valuing that which has been made and called worthy by God.

Fast-forward to John 1 in the New Testament, where we encounter "the Word" which "became flesh and dwelt among us"—Christ, the son of God, eternally spoken and begotten from the Father—the "true light that gives light to everyone" (John 1:9, 14). By inhabiting a body and a created world from the works of his own hands, Christ was naming the world as good and worthy of saving, despite the fracturing that had occurred when Adam and Eve sinned.

As a scholar of writing and literature, I am constantly humbled by the ways God invites us to participate in his story, to resonate with that imprint of his nature that weaves lines of poetry and value into our being. Paul wrote in Ephesians that "we are his workmanship [Gk. *poiema*] created in Christ Jesus for good works" (2:10). *Poiema* means something made, and I believe God invites us to make because we are made, to "sub-create," as Tolkien wrote about in his wonderful essay "On Fairy Stories."[10]

———————

[10] See María Del Rincón Yohn, "J. R. R. Tolkien's Sub-Creation Theory: Literary Creativity as Participation in the Divine Creation," *Church, Communication and Culture* 6, no. 1 (2021): 17–33.

So, what does all this mean at a practical level? How do these ideas and understandings of God's creative, linguistic nature make their way into my classroom? My teaching involves as much Christian practice, participation, and posture as much as it does doctrine. When I teach freshman writing, I often begin by encouraging my students to start with their own narratives, to trace notions of calling and faithfulness that have led them to our university. When we workshop each other's writing, I ask my students to be charitable readers of each other, to offer positive and critical feedback given out of love for each other and a desire to sharpen each other. I try to create space in our group discussion where everyone feels welcome to share his or her own opinion. Sometimes, too, we celebrate great works of writing, whether Martin Luther King Jr.'s "Letter from Birmingham Jail" or David Foster Wallace's Kenyon College commencement address by reading portions out loud. When my students turn an essay in, I ask them to reflect on both the ways they struggled *and* succeeded in their writing. I joke and tell them to give themselves a pat on the back, and often at least half the class will try to do it.

When I think of the great teachers I have had, I find myself remembering more their attitudes and the atmosphere they created rather than any individual lesson or factoid they shared. So, I want my students to come out of my classroom as more empathetic listeners, recognizing that to win any argument one must first properly know, understand, and care about other opinions. I teach them to recognize the *imago Dei* in each other, the imprint of God, that we are "no mere mortal" but eternal beings as C. S. Lewis explores in his essay "The Weight of Glory." Alan Jacobs, writing on the Russian critic Mikhail Bakhtin, says that the "real initiator [of a conversation] is the person who listens."[11] I hope that my students might go into the world as more loving Christians and skilled writers, confident in what God has called them to.

So much of my discipline, English, is caught up in the deconstructive methods of postmodern critical theory. Now, it is good and God-ordained, I believe, to ask the right questions and use our minds to interrogate the ways we may have failed to understand truth. It is good to look at the world

---

[11] Alan Jacobs, *The Pleasures of Reading in an Age of Distraction* (New York: Oxford University Press, 2011), 54–55.

and notice the systemic and fallen ways in which sin perpetuates itself. Still, I believe that it is more valuable to build something up than to just habitually break things down. To say there is a *telos*, an end for which we do things, rather than an abyss that is all that exists once we have broken everything down. We need a destination, a direction, and the Christian writer can often point us to the fabric of beauty and truth and empathy that is woven into the world by our Creator.

Yet I know that language has its limits, this side of heaven. Part of my calling is to also navigate the space where language fails. We humans are finite, after all, and while God may have the language for suffering, grief, beauty, joy, death, and resurrection, we often fail in our attempts to name that which is often unnameable. As a creative writer and poet myself, I recognize the value of trying to name these experiences, just as Dante tried years ago in *The Divine Comedy*. In the last book, *Paradiso*, the narrator reaches the dwelling place of the Trinity after having made his pilgrimage through the inferno and purgatory. Yet here, Dante wrote that his speech fails to express the beauty of the interconnected triune God. It is the most abstract and unclear moment of his epic spiritual journey, but it is also beautiful in its attempt. We are made better as human beings for having it as literature we can return to as we contemplate the divine.

FURTHER READING

Cole, Graham. *Faithful Theology: An Introduction*. Wheaton, IL: Crossway, 2020.

Krieder, Glenn, and Michael Svigel. *A Practical Primer on Theological Method: Table Manners for Discussing God, His Works, and His Ways*. Grand Rapids: Zondervan, 2019.

Meadors, Gary T., ed. *Four Views on Moving beyond the Bible to Theology*. Grand Rapids: Zondervan, 2009.

Porter, Stanley, and Steven Studebaker. *Evangelical Theological Method: Five Views*. Downers Grove, IL: IVP Academic, 2018.

Putnam, Rhyne. *The Method of Christian Theology: A Basic Introduction*. Nashville: B&H Academic, 2021.

Veeneman, Mary. *Introducing Theological Method: A Survey of Contemporary Theologians and Approaches*. Grand Rapids: Baker, 2017.

2

God

M any times, when we hear about the doctrine of God or read about the doctrine of God, we start with a general concept of "God," and then maybe some attributes that describe this deity. Then, eventually, we learn that Christians worship a triune God: God the Father, God the Son, and God the Holy Spirit. Then we try to shoehorn that doctrine back into what we have already placed under the concept of "God." It might seem natural to think this way, to work from the general notion of God to the God of Christianity. We understand "God" in the abstract, and then move forward to understand the doctrine of the Trinity.

But can we ever know God in the abstract? If what we've learned about divine revelation is true—that the only way we can know anything about God is if he reveals himself to us—can we ever know God in the abstract? If Christianity is true, and it is the triune God of the Bible who reveals himself to us, then we are always being addressed by and coming to know the personal God: God the Father, God the Son, and God the Holy Spirit. That is the beginning of our knowledge of God as Christians. Even though the doctrine of the Trinity is revealed most clearly in the New Testament, even in the Old Testament it is the personal God revealing himself to us. Only from this starting point can we learn about that God. We never learn anything true about God apart from God as Trinity. Therefore, we'll start off with the doctrine of the Trinity, and then move on to understand the attributes of God within that personal and relational context. It is the Christian way.

GOD AS TRINITY

What are we talking about when we talk about the Trinity? You may have heard that the Trinity is not even in the Bible. While that is true in one sense—the word "Trinity" does not appear in the biblical text—it also misleads. While we do not get any clear word, like "Trinity," in Scripture itself, we do get three affirmations, or three things that the Bible does say about God. These three affirmations are impossible to hold together apart from the doctrine that we know as the doctrine of the Trinity. Another way to say that is, while the word "Trinity" does not appear in the Bible, the reality of God as Trinity holds the Bible itself together. Let us walk through these three affirmations.

First, the Bible clearly teaches there is one God. You see this throughout the Old Testament, including one of the most central passages shaping the identity of the Jewish people as they prepared to move into the Promised Land. Deuteronomy 6:4 (ESV) says, "Hear, O Israel, the LORD your God, the LORD is One." The word "hear" at the start is a command, underlying the clear truth this passage is teaching and emphasizing to God's people. This belief in one God separated them from their neighbors and made it impossible for them to simply add their neighbors' idols to their worship. Only God can be worshipped; there is only one God. This does not change in the New Testament either. The early Christians always understood their belief in and worship of Jesus to be consistent with this foundational belief about one God. We will explore this more below, but we have to note it here: We can't say, "Well, the New Testament expands that to help us see that there is actually more than one God." It does not. Christian theology never rejects this affirmation drawn from Deuteronomy 6. That is at least partly because Deuteronomy 6 fits with and extends God's work in creation as explained in Genesis.

Second, Scripture identifies three persons as God. We see this in both the Old and New Testaments, though it is more obvious in the New. At the baptism of Jesus, for instance, we see God the Son coming up out of the water, the voice of God the Father from heaven, and God the Holy Spirit descending as a dove (John 1:32). Jesus casts out demons by the Spirit's power (Matt 12:28), and Jesus prays repeatedly to the Father. Jesus also commanded his disciples to baptize in the name of the Father, the Son, and the Holy Spirit (Matt 28:19), which is a clear statement of equality. In the letters of Paul, the apostle speaks of God the Father, God the Son, and God the Holy Spirit in many of his letter openings, offering peace and blessing (see, for instance, Rom 1:1–6; 1 Cor 1:1–3; Gal 1:1–5). When we look back to the Old Testament with this knowledge, we see places where this is hinted at as well.

Third, throughout the Bible, each of these three persons is equally God. We see this, for instance, in Jesus's command to baptize in the triune Name. Three persons; one Name (YHWH). This trivializes it a bit, but I jokingly tell students, "If you were a basketball player, it wouldn't make much sense for me to wish you a good game, that you might play like Michael Jordan, Kareem Abdul-Jabbar, and Bugs Bunny." You would not put those three in the same sentence. Clearly, in what Jesus is doing, he puts the Father, Son, and Spirit on equal footing.

But how can all three of these statements be true? Is this simple math; that is $1 + 1 + 1 = 3$? Or perhaps $1/3 + 1/3 + 1/3 = 1$? How can $1 + 1 + 1 = 1$? Does logic force us to abandon one or more of these statements? In a sense, this is the very question that early Christians wrestled with as they articulated their beliefs in creeds and confessions, in sermons and letters. We will turn to some of their discussions now to help us understand both what to say, and just as important, what not to say.

Early Christians dealt with this question about the doctrine of God in the realm of worship. The three statements we articulated in a more abstract way above informed two ideas present in early Christian worship: There is one God, and Jesus is Lord. Christians insisted on both of these confessional statements, and regularly included them both in their worship practices. The term "Lord," here, is not merely a title of respect; it is a theological name reserved for God alone. In Judaism, the personal name of God given first at Sinai was so revered that they would not even read it aloud; they would substitute the Hebrew word *Adonai*, translated typically as "Lord" in English and *kurios* in Greek. When the NT writers use this Greek word for Jesus, they point back and identify him with the personal name of God from the Old Testament. There is one God, and Jesus is Lord. In the first few centuries of Christian history, pastors and theologians struggled to relate these two terms, but not because they were seeking to change what Christians thought. Christians already believed these statements, and they understood that salvation depended on them. The task was not to invent theology, but to craft a vocabulary that would aid in articulating how these statements could be true at the same time.

Option one: tritheism. Tritheism denies the first statement, that there is only one God. If you deny that, you end up with tritheism. There are three separate beings who are God. They all possess everything that it means to be a god. A Christianity-influenced tritheism would say something like, "There is one god in the Old Testament, and then we meet another one named Jesus, and then a third called the Holy Spirit."

Before you reject this option out of hand, be careful! Of course, if you know much at all about Christianity, you know that worshipping three separate gods is not Christian. But again, be careful! Do you actually act this way sometimes? With my students, I encourage them to evaluate these options honestly and ask themselves, "When do I lean, at least a little bit, toward this view?" If you imagine Jesus taking on flesh as kind of like going on vacation, and the Father and the Spirit hanging out up in heaven, wondering how Jesus is doing, you might be at least a little bit tritheistic. It is certainly easier to introduce separation between the persons of the Trinity, to think about them a bit separately. On one level, we have to do this in our minds just to focus on each person. But we must do so in a way that reminds us of their fundamental one-ness, as well. It is easy to check the box and say, "I'm no tritheist." But it is harder, and more honest, to ask, "Do I pray like a tritheist sometimes?" Or "Do I think about the relationship between the Father, the Son, the Spirit in a way that actually separates them more than the Bible teaches me they're separated?"

Option two: dynamic Monarchianism. Now, stick with me here. You likely recognized the word "tritheism," but think I might be stretching it a bit far to move to "Monarchianism." Both options two and three are types of Monarchianism, and I want to use the word because it's a helpful word. We are all familiar with the notion of a monarch, a king or queen who rules. These next two options both solve the issue by proposing God the Father as a king of some sort, over the other two persons.

Dynamic Monarchianism makes God the Father God in a higher way than the other persons. This position overemphasizes the idea that there is only one God and redefines how it is that Jesus is Lord. Only the Father is properly God, so the Son and the Spirit are second-rate "divinities" of some reduced sort. They come out from the Father in a way that makes them less. The specific examples of this in the ancient tradition are Arianism and adoptionism. Arianism is the idea that Jesus was a created being. Still God in some sense, still divine in some sense, but not in that eternal, equal-with-the-Father sort of way. Why would someone like Arius say this? Because it is in the Bible. You may have even memorized the verse that speaks of Jesus as "firstborn over all creation" (Col 1:15). Arius used this verse in isolation from its greater literary and theological context to argue that there was a time when the Second Person did not exist.

He failed to see that "firstborn" in this context is not talking about temporal succession but eternal ordering and supremacy. Adoptionism was similar. It is the idea that Jesus was merely a remarkable man whom God chose to adopt as his "son." Divine in some sense, but not divine in the same sense as the Father, and therefore inferior to the Father in key ways.

Option three: modalistic Monarchianism. This idea exalts God the Father, making him the only God and the reality behind the other two "persons." There is one God, but that one God is changing, appearing in different "modes." In the Old Testament, he appears as God, or Yahweh, in the Gospels as Jesus, the Son of God, and beginning in Acts as the Holy Spirit. Three persons, but more like successive characters played by the same person. While dynamic Monarchianism can account for the interaction of the Three Persons in the biblical story, modalistic Monarchianism falls short there. For instance, at Jesus's baptism (Matt 3:13–17; Mark 1:9–11; Luke 3:21–23; John 1:29–33), we see Jesus baptized, the voice of the Father calling from heaven, and the Spirit descending like a dove.

Now that we have talked through three ways to get the Trinity wrong, we will turn to the teaching accepted by the church. This position affirms that there is one God and affirms the second idea too: that Jesus is Lord. It does so by introducing some helpful distinctions focused on relationships. By getting a grasp of these ideas, we might not become Trinitarian experts (beware the person who claims to be a Trinitarian expert!), but we can avoid being heretics, which is a noble goal for anyone teaching anything in a Christian context.

We can begin to understand something of what it means that God is Trinity by considering the eternal relationships in which the divine persons exist, while also seeing that the fact that there are relations indicate more than one person.

First, let's consider the language of essence and persons. In the early church, pastors and theologians began to develop ways to talk about the "oneness" of God—the very being and existence of God that is one—using the term "essence." I sometimes tell students to imagine that you could make a list of every characteristic that is required for God to be God. Everything on that list would be shared in its entirety by the Father, Son, and Spirit. They do not split the list up, and it isn't that one person might be better at some of the aspects of being God than the others, so they team up to increase their excellences and perfections. The Father is God. The Son is God. The Spirit is God. Fully, without loss. "Neither blending the persons, nor dividing their essence," as the Athanasian Creed has it.

It is still the Father who is God, the Son who is God, and the Spirit who is God. Scripture introduces each of these three persons as God, and they cannot be blended or reduced to one or another. So how do we talk about the differences, or distinctions between them, if we can even introduce those words without dividing God? Traditionally, the answer has been in their names and in the relationships those names indicate. The Father begets the Son—but not at a certain time, as though there was a time before he was born. The Father begets the Son eternally. "Begets" here does not point to a particular moment in time but to a relationship—the Father-Son relationship—that eternally defines the First and Second Persons.[1] The Holy Spirit proceeds from the Father and the Son.[2] This "procession," like "begetting," isn't something that starts or stops, but that eternally characterizes God.

Another way to get at these realities is through the language of "community of relations." In other words, it is the relationships between the First, Second, and Third Persons that determine their names and their existence as persons. The Father is the Father, which means the Father begets the Son, and the Spirit proceeds from the Father and the Son. What is it that makes the Father and the Son different? The Father begets the Son. What makes the Spirit different? The Spirit proceeds from the Father and the Son. It does not have anything to do with levels of divinity, or timelines of existence, or anything like that. It's all about eternal relationships that define the persons in their equality and existence always already together. The Father did not at some point become Father; that would be a change, and God does not change. The Son did not begin to be, because God is eternal and has no beginning. The Spirit didn't suddenly start proceeding, because that would be moving from something static to something active, and God does not begin to do anything. These are truly mysteries for us, because they are unlike anything else we experience in this world of time, change, and sin.

---

[1] See for instance the Nicene Creed, which speaks of Jesus as the "only begotten Son of God."
[2] You may be aware that "and the Son" points to a long-held debate between Eastern and Western Christians as to how to define the Spirit's relation to the Father and the Son without diminishing him. An introductory book such as this is not the place to chase those debates, but you can look into the "Filioque Controversy" if you find ancient debates invigorating.

Many Christians have turned to analogies to make some sense of these mysteries. You may have heard some of these analogies. For instance, water is water, but it can be vapor, liquid, or ice. A man can be a father, a son, and a college professor. An egg has a shell, white, and yolk, and all are the egg. A clover has three leaves. We must use caution here, and some refuse using analogies at all because of the problems we run into with them. I'm sure you see them: water is not simultaneously vapor, liquid, and ice (except under extreme conditions that our physical science colleagues might regale us with). The shell of the egg is not fully "egg," but only part. Same with the leaves of a clover. In other words, each of these analogies, when pressed, ends up becoming an analogy for a heretical understanding of the doctrine of the Trinity! Yet, instead of rejecting them in their entirety, we simply need to be aware of how they help and how they do not. No analogy is going to be a perfect analogy for the triune God. But these analogies can help us wrap our minds around unity and distinction. In other words, an analogy might help us remember the unity between the persons if we are careful not to follow the analogy too far and introduce too much separation into our view of God. Analogies are limited and can be useful if we understand their limitations and don't press for one perfect analogy for the mystery of the doctrine of the Trinity.

ATTRIBUTES OF GOD

God reveals himself to us in the Bible as Trinity: Father, Son, and Spirit. But he also tells us more about himself, about what he is like. These "attributes of God" arise from direct statements as well as from the biblical narrative itself. Remember, we do not begin with an abstract list of qualities that define a god, and then see if the God of the Bible measures up. Rather, we recognize that the only way we can ever make such a list is in worshipful response to a God who has chosen to enter into relationship with us and reveal himself to us. As we treat the attributes of God briefly here, we must continue to come back to this idea: God is not an abstract list; he is Trinity in unity, revealing himself to the world he has made and is redeeming.

Theologians typically divide the attributes of God into the communicable and incommunicable attributes. The distinction hinges on humans being created in the image of God. We will get to that idea in more detail later, but for now we can simply note that this means there is something that God shares with humans in his creating us in his image. We are *like* God in certain, partial ways. These are the communicable attributes. At the same time, we are not God; we are *unlike* him in very important ways too. These are the incommunicable attributes. This term draws from an older definition of "communicate": to make common. God makes certain attributes common between humans and himself.

God's incommunicable attributes are those that are not true of humans, even in partial or analogical ways. We will consider five of these attributes, grouped in three ways: how God relates to himself and creation, how we think about God and change and suffering, and how God relates to space and time.

In relation to himself and creation, God is simple and self-existent. The doctrine of divine simplicity is easily misunderstood—it certainly does not mean that God is easy to understand! Instead, it means that God's attributes are identical with his being, and God is not made up of separate parts, as though we could divide him out. On one hand, this comes out of the fact that God is spirit (John 4:24). On the other hand, simplicity reminds us how to think properly about all of God's attributes. His attributes are different ways of viewing or speaking about his one, undivided, divine essence or being. His attributes are not separate parts of God, potentially in disagreement with one another. For example, when we come to God in prayer and ask forgiveness for our sins, our hope is not that the "gracious side" of God will win out over the "judgment side" of God. This violates who God reveals himself as in Scripture, and it creates problems in our relationship with God if we miss this attribute. Not only is God simple, he is also self-existent. In theological terms, this is the doctrine of "aseity." God does not depend on anyone or anything else for the fact or quality of his existence. God does not relate to the world because he lacks something or needs something. Rather, God created the world out of his own abundant and overflowing grace, and he chooses to relate to it out of the same. God does not need the world, and God does not need humans. While this might initially seem off-putting in our culture, consider the opposite. A god who is bored, so he creates the world? A god who is lonely, so he makes friends? No, the triune God exists eternally in perfect relationship as Father, Son, and Spirit. He is not divided or dependent.

How does God relate to change and suffering within this world he has made and among these people he has created and chosen to relate to? According to the doctrine of immutability, God does not change. And according to the doctrine of impassibility, God does not suffer. But if we take Scripture as our guide, how do we square these attributes with the fact that God changes his mind (Exod 32:14)? Many different factors come into play here.[3] First, we must remember that sometimes God reveals himself in ways that take into account what it looks like from a human perspective. With Moses, it certainly looked as if God "changed his mind." But instead, the circumstances God was responding to had changed; God himself remained the same and unchanging. In fact, it is this very immutability of God that Moses counts on as he urges God to be gracious. Furthermore, when we think about change, we must remember that we are talking about who God is—God does not change. He does not become better, because he is perfect, and he cannot become worse, because he is holy. God does not change. When it comes to considering suffering, the challenge is different. We often consider suffering as something to do with pain or emotions. God is spirit, so we can move pain to the side. (We will talk about Jesus's suffering on the cross when we learn about the doctrine of Christology.)

What about emotions? In the worldview of the Bible, emotions are also seen as bodily responses to physical events. In some ways, we have come full circle to this view, because our culture often explains emotions through various physiological responses. But in the ancient world, to have emotions meant to have a body, and God does not have a body, so God does not experience emotions. If we shift the language a bit, we might better understand this. What Scripture teaches is that God is never overcome by emotions in such a way that he changes who he is. God is never overwhelmed and acting "out of sorts" or out of character. Scripture clearly teaches that God is love (1 John 4:8), that God hates sin (Ps 5:4), and that God can be angry, though he is slow to anger (Ps 103:8). Yet, these examples are analogical human descriptions about God's consistent character in a changing and often evil world, not a result of God's "blood boiling" or something like that. God's immutability and impassibility are a result of his simplicity, and that is a good thing.

When we talk about God's relationship to space and time, we speak of his omnipresence and eternity. Space and time are both God's creation. As such, God transcends both. He cannot be contained by either space or time. God fills

---

[3] For a more in-depth treatment here, see R. B. Jamieson and Tyler R. Wittman, *Biblical Reasoning: Christological and Trinitarian Rules for Exegesis* (Grand Rapids: Baker, 2022), chap. 4.

heaven and earth (Jer 23:23–24). These are vast mysteries, especially as we grow to learn more about both space and time in disciplines such as physics.

The attributes that God shares with those created in his image are his communicable attributes. We hold them in similar (or analogous) ways, though not in the exact way that God holds them, because he holds them as God, and we hold them as dependent creatures—and sinful too. God's communicable attributes include characteristics such as wisdom, knowledge, power, holiness, righteousness, justice, jealousy, wrath, goodness, love, and mercy.[4] We can understand these to some degree at face value, but two from this list are potentially difficult for us: justice and jealousy. To say that God is just does not mean that there is some external standard by which we measure God and determine him to be just. Rather, we recognize that because of the doctrine of simplicity, God's being is identical with justice. "Justice" is a way we talk about God's entire being, who he is, was, and will be. We must recognize that human justice at its best participates in or points to this God who is just. Regarding jealousy, it is vital to realize that we most often experience sinful versions of this attribute in humans. To be called "jealous" is not usually a compliment. When speaking of God, however, jealousy points to the fact that God, as the only independently existing, eternally perfect being, is rightly concerned with his glory. All that he has created depends on recognizing his glory for our own flourishing, so God's jealousy and our flourishing line up because of the type of God he is and the type of creatures we are.

CONCLUSION

No book chapter can plumb the depths of the doctrine of God. But this has gotten us off to a start. The God of the Bible is not an abstract list of divine qualities, but an eternally existing community of relations—Father, Son, and Spirit. This great mystery will always elude us, even if God has made himself comprehensible to a certain degree for his creatures. When we begin to talk about the attributes of God, we must return continually to Scripture to remind ourselves that these attributes describe a God who is at work in the world redeeming a people for himself. Now we are ready to begin to think about his creation.

---

[4] Michael Horton, *Pilgrim Theology: Core Doctrines for Christian Disciples* (Grand Rapids: Zondervan, 2011), 83.

History and the Doctrine of God
BLAKE MCKINNEY

Humanity is not the author of its own story. Since the beginning of human history, people have sought to grasp control and determine meaning contrary to God's revelation. We live in a Romans 1 world in which God's eternal power and divine nature are clearly displayed for all to see, but people have sought their own way and "claiming to be wise, they became fools" (Rom 1:22). This rejection of God as the author and sustainer of all things is evident in the field of history. In place of the all-wise, all-powerful, triune God who oversees all creation by his sovereign providence, historians have proffered innumerable causal explanations for who we are and how we got here. In so doing, they have ignored the personal, benevolent Creator and offered impersonal, oppressive forces, such as class, gender, race, and a myriad of other materialistic causes. While these modes of analysis gain traction because they help us understand different facets of human history, none is sufficient individually to interpret humanity's past.

How should Christian historians respond? Should we reject all "worldly" models of historical analysis and change all course titles from "History" to "His-Story"? This too would prove problematic. No historian can know the mind of God or speak with confidence about God's purposes in every given historical event. Rather than attempt to merge the offices of prophetic interpreter and historian, Christian historians are free to utilize more than one methodological framework. To borrow language from Augustine, Christian historians may plunder "the treasures" of secular history where they are "appropriate to the service of the truth."[5] They are able to wield a variety of forms of analysis, because they are primarily committed to a Christian worldview and not a particular methodological system.

Presuppositions matter. The biblical presuppositions of Christian historians provide a solid foundation for outstanding historical work. There is truth, and it can be known. Human history has an end-goal. Every single human is an inherently valuable bearer of the image of God. Human authorities derive

---

[5] Augustine, *On Christian Teaching*, trans. R. P. H. Green (Oxford: Oxford University Press, 1997), 64–65. In other editions, see Augustine, *On Christian Teaching*, 2.40.

their power from God's sovereign will. These assertions fly in the face of much historical work, but with this firm foundation Christian historians can utilize a range of methodological frameworks to tell the varied history of God's image-bearers on earth.

Christianity itself is rooted in history. Our faith stands or falls on historical assertions—most importantly that Jesus Christ bodily rose from the dead. The study of history provides unique possibilities to trace the outworking of biblical truth over the millennia, and Christian historians have the opportunity to highlight God's working through his image-bearers in a variety of ways. One such possibility is through exploring the theme of God's communicable attributes in human history.

This chapter has introduced the distinction of God's communicable and incommunicable attributes. There are many ways in which we may identify the outworking of God's communicable attributes in human history. God the Creator has made humans as fundamentally creative beings. The history of science, technology, and the arts tells the story of God's image-bearers following the Creator's example. God imbued his image-bearers with unique reasoning and communicative abilities, which are evident through the study of the history of ideas and philosophy. God is holy and just. Political and legal history provide vistas for human pursuits of a more just society. Furthermore, the study of history prompts us to intellectual humility. God has made himself known, and yet human reason is incapable of fully understanding God. Likewise—in an admittedly imperfect analogy—much of human history can be known and understood, but there will always remain mysteries that we can never unravel.

History provides a wonderful opportunity to demonstrate God's sovereign rule of the world through the survival of the church. Jesus promised that he would build his church, "and the gates of hell shall not prevail against it" (Matt 16:18 ESV). The study of history reveals the transitory nature of human institutions. Nations, governments, and earthly powers rise and fall at a dizzying rate. Christ's kingdom is the only eternal power. History demonstrates the remarkable survival of Christ's church. It has persevered despite persecution, infiltration, heresy, and every imaginable form of human government. Christian historians are blessed with the opportunity to serve their fellow believers by reminding them of God's faithfulness through the ages. As every generation trumpets some social, political, or cultural development as the nadir of human civilization, Christian historians can gently remind them that Christ's church has faced dark days before and the gates of hell did not prevail then, neither will they today or tomorrow. God does not change, and Christian historians can serve their fellow Christians by bearing witness that God's glory, sovereignty, and faithfulness are the same yesterday, today, and forever.

It has been a joy to explore these connections with my students now that I have transitioned from a state university to a Christian institution. It is a blessing to walk through an Ancient History survey course with students demonstrating external evidence for the truthfulness of Scripture. Most of the content of my lectures on ancient Sumerian or Egyptian religions has not changed much. What has changed is how I conclude these lectures. I highlight for my students the fact that these gods once seemed dominant and unassailable in those cultures, but now they are consigned to historical and archaeological study. Whereas only a small minority worshipped our God then, he is still worshipped today while their idols crumble. Likewise, in my other classes I can point to God's protection of the church through a variety of challenges. History may not repeat itself, but historical evidence of God's sustaining protection of his people amid past persecutions, seasons of plague, and scandalous behavior of notable Christians serve as helpful reminders that Christ remains on his throne, and nothing will change that.

Related Scripture

Exodus 34:5–7
Psalm 19:1–14
Psalm 139:1–12
Isaiah 6:3
Isaiah 46:8–11
Isaiah 57:15
Matthew 3:13–17
Mark 12:32
1 Corinthians 1:18–31
1 Corinthians 8:6

FURTHER READING

Bray, Gerald. *The Doctrine of God*. Downers Grove, IL: IVP, 1993.

Carter, Craig. *Contemplating God with the Great Tradition: Recovering Trinitarian Classical Theism*. Grand Rapids: Baker Academic, 2021.

Erickson, Millard. *God the Father Almighty: A Contemporary Exploration of the Divine Attributes*. Grand Rapids: Baker Academic, 2003.

Feinberg, John S. *No One Like Him: The Doctrine of God*. Wheaton, IL: Crossway, 2006.

Packer, J. I. *Knowing God*. Downers Grove, IL: IVP, 1993.

Peckham, John C. *The Doctrine of God: Introducing the Big Questions*. New York: T&T Clark, 2019.

Sanders, Fred. *The Deep Things of God: How the Trinity Changes Everything*, 2nd Edition. Wheaton, IL: Crossway, 2017.

Ware, Bruce, ed. *Perspectives on the Doctrine of God: Four Views*. Nashville: B&H Academic, 2008.

3

Creation

While we are starting a new chapter here, note that we are not exactly leaving behind the doctrine of God. Rather, what we understand as creation is only true insofar as we come to understand creation as a gracious act of God. Creation can only be understood as something that God has done, something he is present with. Creation is obviously not God, but we cannot consider creation apart from God. Or, to put it another way, we do not begin to think about the doctrine of creation by ceasing to think about the doctrine of God. In the Apostles' Creed, for instance, we recite that we believe in one God, "creator of heaven and earth." It is there, in our identifying God as Creator, that we begin to talk about the works of creation.

Additionally, as we enter the doctrine of creation, we are entering an arena where Christians find a lot of disagreement. In what follows, I will not attempt to adjudicate these disputes. Instead, I want to focus on what Christians do agree on and use those agreements as a more promising framework or tether for the disagreements. That God personally created the world, for instance, provides the proper framework for any discussion of the age of the earth. Sometimes in our haste to argue about important, engaging topics, we can take for granted and then actually abandon the common ground that we have. That common ground can provide us the most promising place from which to build our understanding, whatever direction we end up taking.

First, Christians agree that God created the universe out of nothing. You may have heard the Latin phrase for this concept: *creatio ex nihilo*. This is rooted in Gen 1:1, which speaks of God creating all things. Christians have interpreted those early verses differently, some seeing God creating some sort of mass, and then giving form to that mass (which explains the idea of "hovering over the waters"), while others argue that phrases like that are just the ancient poetic way of speaking about nothingness. We see this same concept in places like

Psalm 33, which emphasizes that God made everything—the heavens, their host, in other words, as "far out" as the writer could conceive—by the breath of his mouth. John brings this back up at the beginning of his Gospel, as he explains the eternal Son, the Word, being that through whom "all things were made," excluding nothing (John 1:3). Hebrews 11 speaks to this same reality: by faith we understand that the worlds were prepared by the Word of God, so that what is seen was not made from things which are visible. This idea of God creating the universe out of nothing comes out of passages like that and relates to some things we talked about when we were discussing the attributes of God, the eternity of God. Remember, God alone exists on his own, and God alone exists outside of time, which means everything else is dependent on God for its existence. God created the universe out of nothing.

We also see that the work of the Son and the Holy Spirit are involved. We need to remember, even as we talk about creation, that we are talking about the triune God. In this act of creation, the Father initiates, the Son is the one through whom all is made, and the Spirit is completing, filling, giving life to this creation. We see that in places like Genesis 1 and Job 33. Psalm 104:30 (ESV) says, "When you send forth your Spirit, they are created." Even when we think of the very beginning of Genesis, of creation, we cannot separate our thinking about God from our thinking about the triune God. The Father is the originator, the Son is the One through whom creation is created, and the Spirit is the One by and in whom the completing, filling, and giving of life comes.

Second, creation is distinct from, but always dependent upon, God. This relates to God's transcendence: Transcendence is this idea that God is far above the creation and that he is greater than the creation. He is independent of the creation. It's hard to even define God's transcendence, because we tend to resort to spatial metaphors to do so: God is "above" or "beyond." But transcendence is more than that, because it means God exists independently over anything by which to measure "over" or "above"! That's a good reminder of our limitations, even of our language. At the same time, we must remember God's immanence. God is not one who has remained "above" or "distant," but one who has drawn near, through his tri-personal creative activity and ultimately in the sending of the Son. He truly is, as one of his names in the Old Testament reminds us, "Immanuel," God with us.

This piece of Christian agreement also reminds us that several explanations of the world fall short. Materialist explanations of the universe fall short.

Materialist explanations say that the physical world is all there is. Everything can be explained by natural processes, and there's nothing beyond that at all. Our creation is distinct from God. This position also counters dualism. Dualism—in this sense, means that God and the material world have eternally existed side by side—fails to see that creation is always dependent on God as its Creator. This idea of God being distinct from creation, but creation depending on God, deconstructs these ideas. Additionally, this idea is contrary to deism, meaning that God was involved with the creation, but then he left. He set it up, got it working independently, and is no longer involved. The Christian doctrine of creation is that it is distinct from, but always dependent upon God. We will talk more about this in a little bit when we talk about providence, but it is important to note here as well.

Third, Christians agree that God created the universe for his own glory. We see this in Scripture, clearly. Consider Isaiah 43, which tells us that God created humans for his glory. In Psalm 19, we read that the heavens "declare" the glory of God—and they should! In Revelation 4, John speaks of the worthiness of God. Creation shows God's great power and wisdom. As Christians, we can sometimes start to feel a little hesitant about this aspect of the doctrine of creation. The God of the Bible, the God who took on flesh to sacrifice for sin, created for his own glory? That is what Scripture says. We cannot drive a wedge between God's glory and human good—or animal good, for that matter—without fundamentally misunderstanding God and his creation. God does not lack anything that creation should fill a need; no, it is not that God needs more glory. Rather, God in his eternal goodness and wisdom, chooses by grace to create, and he chooses by grace to guide that creation to glorify him. God, the Father, Son, and Spirit, takes joy and delight in what he chose to make.

Fourth, God created a very good world. The refrain, "and God saw that it was good," chimes throughout the account of creation in Genesis 1. From a Christian background, we can take this for granted. But Israel's neighbors—and today, many of our neighbors—do not believe this. In the ancient world, many explanations of why the world existed were rooted in violence and bloodshed, and they also had very low views of the value of humans. Israel's God creates out of an overflow of goodness and grace, not out of violence like Israel's neighborhood idols. But what about our neighbors? Today, many explanations of the world, and especially human order within it, emphasize some version of a Star Wars explanation: there is light, there is dark, and they are eternally in a battle.

And sometimes, they might be connected in ways that in fact pollute the light. Maybe everything comes down to oppressors and the oppressed, and there is no hope for oppressors. Or maybe the world is just material, and humans must create meaning and achieve significance. This idea in the Christian and Hebrew Scriptures—that God creates something out of goodness and love, and humans are the crown of that creation—sets you up for a very different expectation of what the world should be like.

Now, let us stop to admit that the world as we experience it is far from the very good world that God created in Genesis 1. Here we see a significant way that Christian beliefs are linked together and shed light on each other. When we cover the doctrine of sin later in the book, we will gain a better understanding of how Christians interpret and understand the sin and suffering that is all around us. We might be tempted to two responses. We might abandon the idea that the world is good (for, after all, it's much more comfortable to locate the problem in something "outside" of us, like the world, rather than "inside" of us, like our sinful hearts). On the other hand, we might downplay the suffering and evil around us, always explaining it away without giving it the proper weight and appropriate weeping it merits.

Christians generally agree with those four affirmations. There are legitimate and important questions to explore in relation to science and psychology, for instance, and we'll do some of that at the end of each chapter. But when we explore these questions, we do so best by first understanding the foundation, remaining committed to that, and then beginning to wrestle through the harder cases.

ANGELS

The doctrine of angels is often neglected. This neglect, however, is more evidence of the society that we live in and the views we take for granted than it is about spiritual realities or Christian doctrine. Traditionally, the doctrine of creation includes the treatment of angelic beings because God created them as well. I, for one, grew up hearing more about angels on shows like *Touched by an Angel* than in church, so I must make a conscious effort to reorient my thinking around what Scripture teaches us and not take the easy route of just removing the topic of "angels" from my thinking on Christian doctrine.[1] It certainly isn't controversial in the parts of the world where Christianity is growing the fastest.

While we might not think about angels frequently, Scripture clearly teaches about them, so we should seek to understand what God has revealed. First, angels are persons who were created by God. We see this in places like Psalm 148. We often treat the word "persons" like it is a synonym for "human," but it is not. God is three persons. Angels are persons. Humans are persons. Angels were created by God; they are persons. They have names; they can speak. We see this in places like Luke 1, where an angel speaks to Mary. They are intelligent and they are accountable. We see this, especially, in the book of Revelation. The angelic realm includes all kinds of different angels. There are archangels according to 1 Thessalonians 4 and Jude. These are something like leaders of the angels. We see this in Rev 12:7, where Michael leads the good angels. There are also just "regular" angels. These angels are simply described generally as God's messengers. The seraphim are associated with God's glorious presence (see, for example, Isaiah 6). We also see in Scripture cherubim. These guard the entrance to the garden of Eden in Genesis 3 after the humans are expelled. They are also often described with lots of symbols. We see this in Ezekiel 10, with multiple faces. Other terms are associated with angelic beings as well: terms like "thrones," "dominions," "rulers," and "authorities." We see this in Col 1:16–20. These verses talk about thrones, dominions, rulers, and authorities ultimately being submitted to Christ. But they seem to be some sort of personal powers, but maybe a little different than individual, personal beings. Even the term "powers" is used as well in places like 1 Pet 3:22—these powers are spiritual beings, and they are ultimately submitted to Christ.

Angels are personal beings who serve as messengers of God and sometimes appear in bodily form as part of their work. They are glorious in appearance, usually leading the Bible's authors to strain their language to account for what angels look like, using lots of symbols, metaphors, and exalted language to get at the truth.

Scripture also teaches that fallen angels, under the leadership of a fallen angel named Satan, are bent on the ruin of humanity. We are not given a lot of details about how these angels fell, or about Satan in particular, beyond their

---

[1] Graham Cole's excellent book *Against the Darkness: The Doctrine of Angels, Satan, and Demons* (Wheaton, IL: Crossway, 2019) confronted my neglect in this area and spurred me to remedy it in my class based substantially on his work.

reality, their work against God, and the certainty of their eventual defeat and subjugation to Christ's lordship. We know enough to believe in them, to take them seriously, but not to fear them because of Christ's superiority.

For understanding what Christians believe, we need to boil it down a bit here, so that we do not get distracted by the many things we might want to know about angels (or that we have heard about angels) that we simply don't know because God hasn't chosen to reveal it to us. What we must recognize is that spiritual beings, such as angels and fallen angels or demons, are real, they are persons, and they are active. We aren't to fear them or be unduly interested in them. But we also are not to deny their reality by drifting toward our culture's materialistic explanation of everything. We need to be willing to suffer embarrassment for our belief in angels, because we believe God's Word.

GOD'S WORK IN GOD'S WORLD: QUESTIONING SOVEREIGNTY AND FREEDOM

When we consider the relationship between God and his creation, we do not limit ourselves to "God as Creator" as though the created world is now on its own. Yes, God is Creator of all, and the Bible presents God's creative work as finished—thus his rest on the seventh day. But how do we understand God's ongoing relationship with this world that he has made? We will explore providence and three related concepts that help us grasp this better: preservation, concursus, and governance.

We have already said that God is intimately involved with his world. Providence is talking about how God is continually involved with all created things. Three concepts help us flesh out the forms that God's providence takes.

First, God *preserves* all things. He is the reason for existence, not just the reason for something *beginning* to exist, but for its *ongoing* existence. Paul speaks of all things held together in Christ (Col 1:17). In Hebrews, we receive the image of Christ upholding the universe (Heb 1:3). These verses remind us that, even as we discover the material ways that the created world continues to exist, these stabilizing elements do not exist outside the lordship of Christ; rather, they are the often beautiful, complex, created means *by which* Christ holds all things together. In other words, God's preservation does not mean we deny the material realities that we can see. Instead, it means that we recognize there is more to reality than we can materially see. Christ is not in competition with the laws of nature.

Second, a stranger term: *concursus*. This is the idea that God cooperates with created things in every action. In other words, when we think of any part of creation doing what it does, God is always already working along with it, holding it in being (preservation) and working in it. God gives genuine power to created things to act in accordance with their (and our) nature as created beings, but he does not do that by "giving up" his role as God, sovereign over all things.

Let us dwell here for a moment. Sometimes we experience the challenge of whether God is "in control" or if we are "in control." Often, we experience this as though there are 100 "control points" to go around, and we must figure out how they are split. Does it go 50/50? Do humans have to have 100 for us to be truly free? Well, what about social factors, things outside our control? Do those things get points? The notion of concursus breaks that problem: because of the Creator/creature distinction (God is God and Creator, we are not), he is always completely in control, and created things are also always in control as well. In other words, to say God is in control does not mean that we are not responsible, or that we have no control. Instead, to say God is in control is simply another way of saying that he is God, he is transcendent, he is sovereign. When we speak of our own freedom, we recognize that we have the appropriate control afforded to created things by our Creator. There is not a divine-human competition in the arena of control. God can be 100 percent God, and we can be 100 percent human. Perhaps it will be simpler if we focus away from humans and instead consider other things that God has made.

We see this with inanimate creation. Psalm 148 tells us that God brings fire, hail, snow, and frost. My favorite example is Ps 104:14: God causes the grass to grow. This example puts it all on the table for us modern Christians with our scientific explanations. I am no scientist, but even I know that photosynthesis causes the grass to grow. Is being Christian in the modern world a game of Mad Libs, where we remove "God" from verses and stick new processes in once we discover them? Do we need to change this psalm? No, of course not! Our discovery of photosynthesis does not mean that Ps 104:14 is wrong; God still causes the grass to grow. But we have discovered the created cause by which God sovereignly rules over my lawn. And we do not wonder, "Well, is grass really even grass then, if God causes it to grow?" No, this relationship between the Creator and the lawn is an appropriate relationship for Creator and creature to have. God causes the grass to grow. Photosynthesis causes the grass to grow. Those are not separate processes, but ways of talking about the Creator's work in, with, and among true causes within his creation.

Scripture extends this to the rest of creation too. We see this with animals. God feeds the animals (Ps 104:27–29). Not one sparrow falls without the Father's will (Matt 10:29). We even see it with seemingly random or chance events, the casting of lots, the rolling of dice. There are also events that are fully caused by God and fully caused by the creature. There are levels of causation here, and the divine causes, invisible and behind the scenes. The created cause is discernible; we can see it. But at the same time, we do not put them in competition. Creatures can do appropriate and created things according to their kinds, being the kind of thing that they are created to be. While at the same time God remains in control over that, not because he is making it all happen in the primary way or to the exclusion or resistance of the creature, but because of the integrity of his creation. We even see this in politics: the Bible says God makes nations great and destroys them (Job 12:23; Ps 22:28). If you have studied history or political science, you also know that there are very particular historical sequences we can understand to contribute to the rise and fall of nations. This extends to the aspects of our lives: God gives us our daily bread (Matt 6:11) and fashions the hearts of all (Psalm 33). In Scripture we are told over and over that God does something, and then we are shown—over and over—that same thing as something we do. God is not confused in what he reveals there. He is revealing that he is God, he is sovereign, the creation is real, and the creation is free to operate as appropriate for created things. This is true for the grass, and it is true for the physical mechanism of casting lots, and it is true of human life. (Though, side note: this will get more complicated when we introduce the doctrine of sin.)

The third term that helps us flesh out providence is more familiar: *governance*. The notion of God's governance is that God has a purpose, and he guides all things to that purpose. This is Paul's point in Rom 8:28. God works all things out for the good of those who love him. Governance does not mean we know exactly how God is going to accomplish what he has promised, or that we will know how particular events fit into that ultimate plan. But it does remind us that Scripture shows us a God who has a plan, a God who has made promises, and a God who has kept and will keep them.

Providence, then, is God's continued involvement with creation. He preserves it; he is holding it together. He is always acting in, among, and with his creation. He guides it towards his good and desired end. Each of those categories is important. We are more comfortable with the first one (providence) and the third one (governance). The middle one (concursus) is one of the most challenging theological concepts that we will encounter, but we need it to understand how God is God and the creation is the creation, including us. As we explore the world through the different disciplines within a Christian university, we will certainly find details on which we disagree, but these concepts give us the room to understand how we can find genuine causation within creation without saying, "Well, God must have just created this and walked away." God is a personal God who draws near the world he has made. Providence is one way of talking about that closeness, and Christians have always heard God's providence as good news. It is only in modern times when we are tempted to begin to think things might be better if, say, we were sovereign. Or maybe if scientists could be sovereign. No; God is sovereign, and that is good news.

QUESTIONING SCIENCE AND FAITH

What about areas of disagreement among believers? The doctrine of creation often stirs up the perceived conflict between science and faith, or science and the Bible.

First, we should not feel the need to defend the Bible against the findings of modern science. God can and will defend himself and his Word. When we find ourselves in discussions that seem to pit God's Word against God's world and our understanding of it according to the best tools and thinking we have, we must realize that our unfettered zeal in defense of the Bible is sometimes bubbling out because, deep down, we feel sorry for the Bible and think we had better come to its defense. When we put it out that baldly, we would reject that idea. But I am convinced that sometimes that is where the heat comes from on these issues. There is certainly a place for apologetics and for explaining what the Bible really says on certain issues. We should "defend" God's Word as God's Word. But we should not act as though the Bible's livelihood depends upon our brilliant arguments. The Bible is not in a jam that needs juvenile trickery to escape.

Second, we should not feel the need to downplay the power of science or fuel suspicion of scientists. There can be a problem with scientism, which essentially outsources every possible claim to knowledge to what the scientific method can adjudicate. That's a problem, because the world God created exceeds the world scientists can measure. But we must remember that science can (and should) flourish within a Christian view of the world. In other words, we should be more aware of good science as a Christian practice, rooted in a deep understanding of the doctrine of God. Modern science did not develop to contradict the Bible; it developed because early modern scientists believed that Scripture spoke of a regular world created by a good God, a world that could be studied and known.

Third, we must remember that our theological understanding and our scientific understanding both remain partial and flawed. We will expand on the effects sin has on knowledge when we cover the doctrine of sin, but at this point note that even if we just consider humans as humans—even without taking sin into account—we can know God and we can know God's world as creatures, not perfectly as only God himself can know it. In other words, we should not be surprised when our limited knowledge of God and our limited knowledge of the world seem to be in conflict. This becomes even more exaggerated and difficult when sin comes into the picture.

Fourth, we should not make difficult issues like this one divide Christians or become litmus tests for what it means to be a good Christian. You can probably immediately think of which side "good Christians" fall on with various issues. One thing we need to realize—and help students realize—is there are people much godlier than I who disagree with me on a particular issue, such as the age of the earth, and there are people much smarter than I who disagree with me on this issue too. In other words, we must resist the tendency to approach science and faith questions with the attitude that "holy Christians who really listen to the Bible believe X," or "Christians who actually use their God-given brains believe Y." It is not that simple, and when we encourage students to develop those sorts of assumptions, we do a disservice to them and to the unity of the church.

This conflict that we feel between science and faith is more about our own conflict between darkness and light than it is a conflict between God and the world that he has made. It should humble us, remind us of a limitation of our own understanding, and drive us in submission and humility to the cross for all our understanding.

CONCLUSION

This chapter has likely done what I hope this entire book will do: raise more questions than it answers. I don't hope this because I don't want to give you answers; I do. I think we have covered some clear answers here in what Christians do agree about the doctrine of creation. These agreements give us the boundaries for faithful Christian dialogue and exploration of difficult issues that we confront in this complex and glorious world that God has created. I hope at the very least it will help us ask better, more interesting questions, even as we acknowledge that our answers to some of these questions will not determine our faithfulness or intelligence.

Art and the Doctrine of Creation
HAELIM ALLEN

At the very beginning of Genesis, the triune God first reveals himself to us as a creator, or rather the Creator. He created all things and every being, which all were at first perfect and good. As created beings made in his image, humans also create. This is evident throughout all human history. However, we do not create in the perfect world of Eden but rather in a fallen one, and our existence since then and before the new heavens and the new earth entails the imperfectness of who we are and what we create. As an artist who is an imperfect Christian, this in-between space is keenly felt. But shall we then wait until the world is renewed to perfection to start creating or appreciating the numerous manifestations of art? Of course not! God's presence, our Immanuel, is with us here and now, and he is ever-present in this reality. I dare not think what it would be like without his beauty and presence.

Creating with clay, paint, wood, or any of the bounteous gift of materials he has endowed to us, I am honored and humbled that God would entrust us with these portions of his generative act of creation. We participate in and engage with his creation as we partake in making (and not just in visual art!). As an artist, it is a privilege to manifest his love for his creation in the imaginative spaces of the realm of visual art. In our acts of creating and appreciating, even in the here and now as well as the not yet (be it paintings, works of installation, drawings, and such), we do so with the faculty and imagination given to us from God. The artists' participation in God's creative act is a gift to all humanity, and it is part of the ongoing generative act from the very beginning. As a Christian, the beauty found in his creation and the continuing acts of creation by artists should be celebrated.

This is not to say that all of what we do and make should be celebrated as being worthy or good. There are challenging aspects in the artworld for makers and appreciators alike, especially from a Christian faith perspective. In many ways, the art world refracts issues found in general culture. And since much of the art mirrors and reflects society and culture in a visual manner, tensions arise especially with artworks that do not celebrate beauty, truth, or goodness. This in no way excludes challenging works that prompt or even provoke the viewer to desire a more beauteous and truth-filled world. When the art world celebrates works that are ugly in content (e.g., subject matter, ideology like nihilism, objectification of person/s, or general crudity and lewdness); or poorly crafted works (not just in construction but also in conception and fruition); then it is very difficult to find beauty in addition to what is good and true in such works, and in an ultimate sense, to even celebrate his presence in such examples. However, from my perspective, most works of art are for the good of all, though many might not go beyond being puzzled by the visual expressions throughout the centuries, especially in the contemporary era.

As a contemporary artist, I also find it difficult to relate to my Christian faith community, since often, fine art (less with the decorative arts) is dismissed as an unnecessary aspect of our daily lives. This attitude by Christians toward visual art, especially of contemporary works, in a sense ignores or dismisses the imaginative spirit found in all human beings as part of our being created in the *imago Dei*. By doing so, it hinders the way we could relate to one another in love and charity, both in the present and for the future as well. Viewing a work of art from a different era or culture is an opportunity to see and understand not only the content or message of the work but also how it testifies to the way it was celebrated by the people whom it reflects. Unfortunately, visual art has become suspect and too readily dismissed in the church. Being an artist in the world but not of it becomes a challenging "in-between" space in which to dwell.

Some aspects of our artmaking that should cause us to celebrate are craftmanship, unity and variety, as well as formal components like color, and much more.

Crafting something well is a generally shared signifier of what is good. If a work of art, functional object, or even a research paper, are crafted well in all their portions, then they are deemed to be good works. In visual art, craftmanship is emphasized in all levels of making. The ability to imagine, problem-solve throughout the generative and making processes, and to manifest a work all display God's reflection of what is good (Genesis 1). Craftmanship exhibits not only the "good" in the visible final product but also in the maker's ability to do such good work. This ability to do so reflects on God himself, since we are made in his image.

As visual artists, we consider many aspects of artmaking to include (not a comprehensive list): design principles, elements of design, concept, and context, all as we generate a work to fruition. One aspect that I consider is color. As a colorist painter, I do not always depict the natural colors dictated by a subject matter. Instead, I may make the colors much more brilliant or subdued, depending on the vision and context of the work being generated. Imagine living in a colorless world. How could we celebrate the changing colors of the leaves (even if they do fall off the trees afterwards), as this alludes to not only the change of seasons but also acts as a reminder of death and renewal? We celebrate him in his creation: the verdant fields, the lavender blue skies with hints of orange during a sunset, and the aqua blues and greens of the water, to list a few relevant aspects.

In design principles, one consideration is (as a set) "unity and variety." Both components relate to the whole in generating works of art. One simple explanation of the principle is that in a composition, artists incorporate both aspects to create a more complex and interesting work. An example found in God's creation: He did not make one type of bird but various kinds. Nor did he make only one type of flower, let alone one type of rose or one visage for all human beings. God's bounteous creativity is visible all around us in various ways, and yet, all reflect unity in design, category, or type. This too reveals something about God and who he is as Creator.

The works of art reflecting such a principle of unity and variety, celebrating foundational aspects of art like color, and with good craftmanship, are those works that reflect God's creation and design. He has and continues to reveal himself, especially through his Word, sacraments, and the "cloud of witnesses," but also through his creation as well. As people of the faith, who love and delight in him, we should contemplate and reflect him and celebrate the many ways in which visual art prompts us to love him, his creation, and our neighbor.

Related Scripture

Genesis 1
Genesis 2:7–23
Psalm 33:6–9
Psalm 104:5–30
Acts 17:24–31
Romans 8:19–22
Colossians 1:15–23

FURTHER READING

Anderson, Gary A., and Marcus Bockmuehl. *Creation ex nihilo: Origins, Development, Contemporary Challenges.* South Bend, IN: University of Notre Dame Press, 2019.

Ashford, Bruce Riley, and Craig G. Bartholomew. *The Doctrine of Creation: A Constructive Kuyperian Approach.* Downers Grove, IL: IVP Academic, 2020.

Fulkerson, Geoffrey H., and Joel Thomas Chopp, eds. *Science and the Doctrine of Creation: The Approaches of Ten Modern Theologians.* Downers Grove, IL: IVP Academic, 2021.

Moo, Jonathan A., and Douglas J. Moo. *Creation Care: A Biblical Theology of the Natural World.* Grand Rapids: Zondervan, 2018.

Stump, J. B., ed. *Four Views on Creation, Evolution, and Intelligent Design.* Grand Rapids: Zondervan, 2017.

Wilson, Jonathan R. *God's Good World: Reclaiming the Doctrine of Creation.* Grand Rapids: Baker Academic, 2013.

4

Humanity

We first encounter the question, What does it mean to be human? in a very personal way: "Who am I?" And we live in a culture that makes this very personal question the foundation of so many things. Issues of identity, the categories that are employed, and the surrounding controversies seem to multiply endlessly. Race. Ethnicity. Sex. Religion. Sports! We might need many of these categories to describe people or to understand some aspects of ourselves. But the doctrine of humanity—or theological anthropology, in more technical terms—goes to the depths of what it means to be human, our shared humanity. We need to understand this shared humanity as fundamental before adding adjectives and qualifiers that divide us.

Even that statement might be controversial in many circles. But Christians have consistently believed there is something fundamental about being human that all humans share. Christians have believed that to be human is not something we create, or that consistently changes, or is fractured. Even when Christians have been inconsistent in their application of the doctrine of humanity in certain historical contexts, Christians have offered an answer to what it means to be human. We can see this answer from different angles by considering different relationships: the relationship with God, the relationship with the self, the relationship with others, and the relationship with the rest of creation. We'll start with the most foundational: our relationship to God.

RELATING TO GOD—*IMAGO DEI*

We get the idea of "the image of God" from three passages in the Old Testament. All three are in the beginning of the book of Genesis. The first and fullest reads: "Then God said, 'Let us make man in our image, after our likeness. And let them have dominion over the fish of the sea and over the birds of the heavens and over the livestock and over all the earth and over every creeping thing that creeps on the earth.' So God created man in his own image, in the image of God he created him; male and female" (Gen 1:26–27 ESV). God roots his decision to create humans in the concept of his image. Second, God refers back to this in Gen 5:1. Before giving the genealogy from Adam to Noah, God reminds the reader that all in this line share in the image of God, in which God had created Adam and Eve.

Third, Gen 9:6 prohibits murder, and God roots the prohibition in the fact that he made humans in his own image. As the revealed logic goes, it is wrong to kill humans because to do that is to marshal an assault on the divine image. Therefore, an attack on humans is an attack on God. Also, it is significant to know that these last two references both occur after the fall, which means that the image of God is not something that is lost in the fall. If it were lost, it would not define the genealogy from Adam to Noah, and it also wouldn't make sense to prohibit murder based on an image that was lost. No, the image of God remains, even after the fall.

Together, these three passages demonstrate that the "image of God" is an important foundational concept for what it means to be human. Even if it is not repeated throughout Scripture, as other themes are, its presence at the beginning of Genesis and the use that God makes of it there, demonstrate its significance. However, these three passages do not make immediately clear what it exactly *means* for humans to be created in God's image, or what "part" of humans is the image.

Christians have wrestled with how to answer this perplexing question. "What is it about being human that reflects God's own identity?"

Christians have given three answers to this question: the image as a substance that makes us like God; the image as a function that we undertake making us like God; and the image as the ability to be in relationship with others. Let us look at each of these, even if briefly.

First, the image of God means a connection to some substance that is alike between God's nature and our nature. In other words, there is some feature or capacity of humans that animals and other elements of creation do not share. Christians have proposed various possibilities: the soul, rationality, the ability to pursue "the good," the ability to love, or some innate sense of God.

Second, the image of God turns to focus on the unique task that humans are given in creation, or the unique function that we play. We see that God gave

Adam and Eve "dominion" (Gen 1:26 ESV). According to this perspective, the image is seen when God-given authority and responsibility are exercised.

Third, the image of God points to the ability to relate and the necessity of relationships. This view starts with God's triune nature, his perfect life as Father, Son, and Holy Spirit. We are relational beings and cannot be truly alone.

Theologians have also regularly pointed to Jesus as the perfect image of God. Jesus is the repairer of the image damaged in the fall. Theologian Richard Lints explains that Paul's Adam-Christ typology from Romans 5 lays the foundation for his arguments in Romans 6 and 8. In those chapters, Paul explains that Christians must be identified with Christ in his death to share his resurrection. In fact,

> the gospel finds itself in seed form, then, all the way back in Genesis 1 when God created humankind in the divine image. As the perfect image, Christ completes the original vocation of humankind and thereby shows humankind who they were originally intended to be. This does not happen, however, without experiencing the cross wherein the power of the idols was broken and death lost its sting. The perfect image not only reveals what redeemed humans will eschatologically be but also loosens the bonds of their present enslavement to the idols they have created.[1]

Clearly, Christ serves as an example of a "repairer." The perfect, sinless One gives us a picture of the image unbroken. By his death on the cross, he also makes the necessary repair possible. In other words, Jesus gives us a picture of what the image of God should be, and he also offers to fix it in us. Our broken images can be mended because of his example and work.

To understand the image of God, we must start with the Old Testament's fundamental—though limited—references and understand the theme in light of the way that Jesus displays this image and re-makes fallen people into it. Bringing these different ways of seeing the image together helps us see something else that God reveals early in Genesis: humans are created for the purpose

---

[1] Richard Lints, *Identity and Idolatry: The Image of God and Its Inversion*, NSBT 36 (Downers Grove, IL: InterVarsity, 2015), 126.

of serving God as co-rulers. God has made us in his image and given us a task to do (what is often referred to as the "dominion mandate"). The image itself is not the task, but they are certainly related. The image makes the necessary task possible and absolutely necessary. This task is not just Adam's alone; it is also Eve's and their descendants', including us. Here we see the various angles for considering the image come together: something substantial aimed at a particular function to be carried out in relationship, all perfected in Christ.

RELATING TO THE SELF: THE HUMAN CONSTITUTION AND FREE WILL

Now let us consider how each person relates to the self. What makes up the human self, and how does that composition impact what we can do? Here we're dealing with such concepts as the soul, spirit, mind, and body. We can lump these together under the idea of "human composition."

We can imagine various ways of relating these "parts" together in our understanding of what makes up the human. Monism argues that humans are one thing, typically defined as physical beings. This view is also called physicalism. Dualism views humans as two things, a soul and a body, that are related in different ways depending on the type of dualism. Trichotomy, finally, inserts a third "part," leading to body, soul/spirit, and mind. In other words, trichotomy tries to hold to a physical component, an intellect, and an emotional/spiritual component.

You might initially think that trichotomy is the biblical view because the Bible refers to (at least) three of these ideas. Jesus, for instance, told us to love God with all the heart, soul, strength, and mind in the Greatest Commandment (Luke 10:27), so he must have at least believed in trichotomy, if not quadotomy! However, it is not this simple, because the Bible refers not to separate parts but to the one human from different angles. Consider "flesh," for example. At first glance we might think this is a "physical body" word, but that is not how it is used. When Paul talked about the problems of the flesh, he was not recommending that if we could simply abandon the physical, all our problems would be solved. Instead, "flesh" is better understood as referring to the human as creature and other times to the human as a corrupted being.

So how are we to consider human composition? We have a few routes by which we can affirm the unity of the human person—however you articulate the constituent parts—while acknowledging the spiritual and physical realities involved. One route is through a type of dualism, one that properly emphasizes the necessary unity between two "parts" in such a way that neither the human body nor the human soul is properly "at home" without the other. Another route is to emphasize the unity through monism—or perhaps we could say a weak physicalism—that identifies something like a higher-order human spirituality emerging out of and made possible by the physical bodies that we are, and the physical elements and processes that are involved. The key with such a monism is to insist that though these spiritual realities are connected to and even in some sense made possible by physical explanations, they are not reducible to the physical explanations alone. Theologian Millard Erickson holds something like this position, dubbing it "modified monism." He emphasizes that we are not bodies *plus* something, but we are also not *merely bodies*. Others use the terminology of "compound unity" to highlight that the "soul" and the "body" are united in an irreducible way, and their separation at death is a tragic break, a break that God will heal, and indeed that only God can heal.

These issues matter because our understanding of what it means to be human helps us better understand the type of hope that God provides us. For instance, if being human means to be some sort of compound unity, irreducibly physical and spiritual, then we can expect salvation to heal all of this. If what really mattered was the spiritual, then maybe salvation just helps us escape from our bodies. But that is not what we see in the Bible. Christians care about the body, and we wait in hope for an embodied eternity. Furthermore, the promise of eternity with God is revealed to us in terms of resurrection and the continuity of personal identity. Any explanation of the relationship of the soul and the body that claims to be Christian must take account of this resurrection hope, embodied eternity, and continuity of identity. Jesus's resurrection was seen as a firstfruits (1 Cor 15:20–23), and Paul said to be absent from the body is to be present with the Lord (2 Cor 5:8) before resurrection (1 Thess 4:16–17) and eternal existence.

Another related aspect here is the notion of free will. There are five general areas where Christians generally agree about this topic, as explained by theologian Marc Cortez. First, humans have free will. Second, humans exercise their free will in ways that make them morally responsible. Third, not all human actions and decisions are meaningfully free. Fourth, free will and divine sovereignty are compatible. And fifth, free will is related in important ways to preceding factors.[2] While different people explain these aspects in different ways, these represent general areas of agreement on this difficult topic.

Books can and have been written exploring the full scope of free will. Such detail is beyond us here, but we can look at two major ways of approaching the problem. Few Christians hold to complete, hard determinism—which rejects free will entirely—so we will skip that one here.

Compatibilists hold that human actions are determined by causes *and* that humans are free and morally responsible for their actions. One reason that some hold this position is because contemporary science continues to demonstrate that creatures are governed by causal laws, so these causes must be accounted for in our understanding of human action and free will. Others look to various biblical and theological arguments that support this position, such as nothing happening outside of God's power (Ps 103:19). Philosophical reasons also lead some to reject other options and land with some form of compatibilism. For example, those who believe in libertarian free will have difficulty in relating any causation to the act of the free will, thus making it seem random.

But how can being caused and being free go together? Compatibilists take different tracks to answer this question. The classic response is that you are free as long as you can choose to do what you want. However, your desires are caused by complex factors (some of which you can control to some degree some of the time). In this approach, God still exercises control over the desires of the heart, and we can operate according to what we want most. Therefore, we are morally responsible.

Another response is called hierarchical compatibilism, which connects truly free actions to our deepest desires. Hierarchical interpretations want to leave room for humans not being morally responsible for actions based on compulsive desires or psychological disorders, and a hierarchy helps make those distinctions. Still others hold that only actions that respond properly to rational considerations are truly free. According to this approach, free actions are the actions that have rationality behind them.

Libertarians, on the other hand, believe that determinism is incompatible with free will. In other words, if there is anything causing the will, then the will is not free. Because everyone knows free will exists, determinism must be false.

---

[2] Marc Cortez, *Theological Anthropology: A Guide for the Perplexed* (London: T&T Clark, 2010), 99–100.

At one level, libertarians take a popular conception of free will that most people assume, and they use that definition to reject determinism. Much like hard determinists, they see no way to reconcile determination and freedom. Hard determinists side with determinism; libertarians side with free will.

Christian versions of libertarianism rely on philosophical reasoning about freedom's definition, but also on biblical texts. For instance, the Bible says that people must choose to follow God (Josh 24:15), and in others God commands people to make choices and expects them to respond (Matt 3:2). Christian libertarians insist that any sort of causation of the will would make such choices and responses programmed and therefore not free. Why would God command something that is programmed?

Like compatibilism, libertarianism includes varieties of nuance. Some thinkers argue that a truly free will cannot have any cause at all other than itself. Most libertarians, however, acknowledge that choices are caused in some way but are not fully determined. In other words, there are past influences (events, character traits, etc.) that can impact a still-freely operating will. Those past events or traits of the person, however, do not render the choice certain or determined. They might play a role, but the will can still go in many directions even taking those causes into account.

We will not likely resolve this debate anytime soon. It also touches on other important doctrines—the doctrine of God (especially his providence) and the doctrine of salvation (how do people choose God?), to name two. The human constitution—and how the human will actually operates—raises confusing questions, but we must not let those questions distract from the basic theological concepts. Humans are not basically souls stuck in physical bodies, but a compound unity of body and soul. We live in a world created by God and under his care and providence, and we make meaningful choices that we are responsible for.

RELATING TO THE OTHER: SEXUALITY

Without doubt, Christianity's traditional teaching on sexuality stands as one of the most controversial elements of Christian doctrine. On the surface, we see controversy surrounding gay marriage and various anti-discrimination laws related to sexuality, but it goes much deeper. In fact, in some ways, a traditional Christian understanding of sexuality is rooted in more fundamental beliefs about what it means to be human, beliefs that also contradict those in the prevailing Western culture. We should not be surprised that Christianity is out of step with the culture on sexuality, because Christianity is out of step with the culture on what it means to be human.

We see sexuality present from the beginning, starting in Genesis 1. There, in verse 27, God creates humans "male and female," even before Genesis 2 explains in more detail. In that chapter, we see that God created Adam first and, seeing that it was not good for him to be alone, God created the woman to be the man's "helper." (This word is sometimes used of God in Scripture, so it does not necessarily imply some sort of inferiority that we might read into it in our context. It's about necessity.) Sexual complementarity is certainly in view, but the passage is about more than Adam needing a counterpart in order to reproduce. Creating humans as "male and female" wouldn't be remarkable or noted if it only meant male and female for reproductive purposes, just like the rest of the animals. Creating humans as male and female receives special attention as something that defines humanity, that tells us something unique about what it means to be human as opposed to what it means to be an animal. While we find maleness and femaleness in the rest of creation, the idea of humans "as male and female" seems to be about more than just reproduction. Adam needs help in more than just that department.

As we begin to discuss the role of sexuality in the doctrine of humanity, let's define some terms. By "sex," scholars typically refer to biological features associated with the designation "male" or "female." While we might think that this refers only to external features such as sex organs, more than that is in view here. These features include people's chromosomes, the hormones that were dominant while they were *in utero*, the kinds of internal and external organs that are developed, and the relative amounts of hormones produced during puberty.[3] The term "gender," on the other hand, varies in usage so widely as to be nearly impossible to understand without careful scrutiny.[4] For some, "gender" simply means social expectations that are associated with one sex or the other, expectations that are often related to biological differences between the sexes.

These definitions might seem to deal with the issues fairly cleanly: biologically determined "sex" is socially shaped into "gender," which is the socially

---

[3] Cortez, 47.

[4] For a recent treatment of the term *gender*, see Abigail Favale, *The Genesis of Gender: A Christian Theory* (San Francisco: Ignatius, 2022), esp. ch. 6.

acceptable way for members of a given sex to live and act. Some see this explanation to be as far as we need to go, but it doesn't adequately deal with various problems, and it also doesn't account for the fact that "gender" is used in such broad and sometimes contradictory ways. First, there are rare biologically ambiguous cases, in which one or more of the biological determiners of sex does not line up with the others. One scholar cites the example of Maria Patiño, who had female genitalia and sought to compete in the Olympics as a female. She underwent testing in 1985, which determined that she had XY chromosomes instead of the female-typical XX chromosomes, and was unable to compete as a female.[5] Such challenging cases force wisdom and discernment in how we understand and deal with these rarer cases.

We also must resist the simplistic idea that biological sex creates all differences, full stop. Social and environmental influences clearly impact the way cultures develop expectations associated with each sex. This then impacts how individual people do or do not meet those expectations. While some aspects of sex-assigned expectations are driven by biological factors, even those aspects are also socially and environmentally influenced.

As Christians, we can recognize that different cultures place different expectations on each sex, and sometimes these expectations differ. (Consider length of hair, for instance.) At the same time, the Christian doctrine of humanity and sexuality clearly stops short of a "strong constructivism," which contends that there is no biological foundation for gender and sexuality at all, and that it all depends on language and culture. Instead, we have to recognize that biological differences in sex underlie our sex-assigned differences in various cultures, but in complex ways that are at the same time impacted by particular cultures. In other words, there is a biological givenness to sex, but our reception and interpretation of that givenness always happen within individual cultures. The relationship between biological sex and culturally defined expectations is complex, which is why we must rely on what God has said about such things. On our own, we struggle to work through the ambiguity, which is why many have given up and simply placed it all at the feet of cultural constructivism.

But how do we think about sexuality from a theological perspective? Theologian Marc Cortez gives us a few helpful options. First, some see sexuality as primarily aimed toward procreation. According to this perspective, the

---

[5] Cortez, *Theological Anthropology*, 51–52.

purpose of sex is reproduction. But this limited view fails to see anything different about human sexuality in comparison to the rest of creation. It fails to see
the value of non-procreative sex and the full humanity of persons who cannot
have children.

Second, others explain sexuality as pointing to God's "fecund nature." In
other words, God is creative, and sexuality is one way that humans "create" by
producing offspring. This position makes human reproduction different from
the rest of creation, but it still fails to see the fundamental importance of sexuality. Additionally, this view runs into issues with potentially making God's creation necessary to his being.

Third, still others view sexuality as marriage or relationality. In their opinion, sexuality demonstrates that humans are relational beings. Unfortunately,
these types of views tend to make sexuality a secondary element of what it
means to be human. This also does not fit well with the importance it is given
in Scripture.

In response to these three possibilities, Cortez prefers to see sexuality as
"bonding." But what does he mean by that, and how is it different than relationality? In this formulation, Cortez includes the strengths of the relation-
ality/marriage view while at the same time emphasizing the significance of
humans as sexual beings. As he puts it, "The sexual human being finds within
itself a desire for another in whom there is both difference and identity." He
continues in his next paragraph, "This drive toward bonding, then, forms the
basis of the connection between human sexuality and the broader importance
of relationality and community for humanity in general."[6] In this way, Cortez's approach views sexuality as central to what it means to be human. At the
same time, it includes space for insights from the other views as expressions of
human sexuality—though not exactly the basic essence of it.

RELATING TO OTHERS: FRIENDSHIP

Humans are open to and need each other, but this fact is not fulfilled only—or
even primarily—with sexual expression. While the human need for relationship finds expression in sexuality, it is also found beyond it. Human relationships more broadly considered can be treated under the notion of "friendship."

---

[6]   Cortez, 65.

First Samuel offers an excellent example of this need with the stories of David's and Jonathan's friendship. According to the text, Jonathan's soul was "knit" to David's, and Jonathan loved David as himself (1 Sam 18:1). When David laments Jonathan's death, he says that Jonathan's love surpassed the love of women (2 Sam 1:26). Some scholars argue that these verses indicate Jonathan and David had a homosexual relationship. But it is much more faithful to the original text (and the entire biblical canon) to see this instead as focusing on the significance of friendship, including the heights to which such friendships can attain. In fact, it is a sign of our own devolution of the category of same-sex friendships that we start suspecting homosexuality any time closeness is described between members of the same sex. David and Jonathan sacrificed for one another, gave gifts to each other, and remained loyal. They liked each other and enjoyed being together. This is but one famous biblical example of what friendship can be.

Friendship provides a category for human relationality that does not include sexual expression but is not deficient because of that fact. While a proper understanding of sexuality sees its unique role in human bonding and openness to the other (as argued above), humans can still relate to one another in other significant ways. Friendship is often taken for granted or ignored, but the need for non-sexual relationships remains an important expression of human relationality and need for community.

RELATING TO THE REST OF CREATION: HUMANS AS THE "CROWN OF CREATION"

Last, we turn to the relationship between humans and the rest of creation to better understand the Christian doctrine of humanity. Scripture gives us clear statements on the place of humans in creation. God has made humans a little lower than the angels, as Ps 8:5 puts it. Paul reminds us in Eph 2:10, humans are God's masterpiece. And as we have already seen in Genesis 1, God created humans in his image and placed them over all of the creation.

Yet, as humans have become more and more aware of the value of the rest of creation and humanity's ability to cause harm to it, some hesitate to define humans so highly. Concern for the environment has led in some cases to elevating the rest of the created order to the same level as humanity. Concern for animals and their rights has led to a similar leveling. In both cases, the

Christian idea of humanity as the "crown" of God's creation has become an embarrassment.

The key with this element of the doctrine is to accept the elevated description of humanity's place in creation, which Scripture gives, but to likewise accept the elevated role and responsibility given as well. Christians must grapple with what faithful stewardship of a beautiful creation looks like, not because it is of equal status as humans but because God has entrusted us with that task. The same goes for animal rights: the answer is not in lowering humanity or elevating the animal kingdom to the same status as those created in God's image. But the treatment of these fellow creatures does matter. Both environmentalism and the animal rights movement can help Christians see past abuses and potential temptations, but the best answers for a way forward do not lie in rejecting the plain sense of the verses we looked at above.

CONCLUSION

The doctrine of humanity is vital to a proper understanding of Christian theology. We cannot understand our own lives without it. However, it is important to remember that when we are talking about humans, we are talking about God's creation. In other words, God must be central to our understanding of what it means to be human. This fact is one reason why we must turn to see what God has to say about humanity in the Bible rather than only looking at what we can figure out about ourselves.

Our understanding of humanity does not stop here, however. To understand where the Bible takes us in the story of salvation, we must seek to understand why salvation is even needed. We'll turn next to understand what Christians mean when we talk about the doctrine of sin.

Exercise Science and the Doctrine of Humanity
ANNA ROSE ROBERTSON

One could consider exercise science a difficult field in which to teach one's faith. After all, science is science. How can one include faith in such a black-and-white area of study? However, the messages our culture is sending to today's generation are in stark contrast to the evidence science provides regarding gender and how God has created us—our similarities and our differences. Exercise science is an area in which faith can be integrated in today's classroom because of how science confirms the teachings of the Bible: males and females are different, *and* both are created in God's image. It is quite ironic that culture is currently sending the message that I may choose my gender and even change my mind on a day-to-day basis; yet science provides ample evidence of the differences in males and females, specifically regarding exercise.

God-given differences between males and females and their adaptations and abilities within exercise is an area of study in which faith can most definitely be integrated. Science and the study of exercise reveal several gender-based differences among males and females (flexibility, VO_2 max,[7] ability to build muscular strength, etc.). The classifications for exercise norms (push-ups, sit-ups, body composition, flexibility, etc.) are different for males and females. Within exercise science, the tests used for measuring health-related components (body composition, muscular strength, muscular endurance, and flexibility) are different for males and females. For example, when measuring upper body strength, females are tested using modified push-ups, and males are tested using full body push-ups. The locations used for measuring fat distribution are also different. Women are measured at the triceps, suprailium, and thigh when measuring body composition using the skinfold method. Alternatively, men are measured at the chest, abdomen, and thigh.[8]

Here are just a few of the exercise-related differences between males and females:

> Males have higher hydration needs than females.
> The VO_2 max of males is approximately 10 percent more than females.[9]

---

[7] VO_2 max is a measurement of how much oxygen an individual can absorb and use during exercise.

[8] Werner W. K. Hoeger et al., *Lifetime Physical Fitness & Wellness*, 15th ed. (Boston: Cengage Learning, 2017).

[9] Robert Murray and W. Larry Kenney, *Practical Guide to Exercise Physiology: The Science of Exercise Training and Performance Nutrition*, 2nd ed. (Champaign, IL: Human Kinetics, 2020), 168.

Females are more flexible than men after puberty.[10]

Females are at a higher risk of tearing their ACLs (anterior cruciate ligament) than are males.[11]

Females have higher body fat than men. In fact, they need more body fat for their bodies to function than do men.[12]

Let us examine each of these facts.

Males have higher hydration needs than females. They need to consume 3.7 liters of water per day, and females need only 2.7 liters of water per day, as recommended by the U.S. Institute of Medicine. Why do men typically weigh more than females? Generally, men have more muscle mass than do females. Why are men able to have more muscle mass than females? Men have twenty to thirty times higher testosterone levels than do females, and testosterone absorbs more water.[13]

The VO_2 max of males is approximately 10 to 15 percent higher than females. Age and training status can be controlled, and most males will still have a higher VO_2 max than females even if their competitive times are slower than females.[14]

Females are more flexible than males. Before puberty, the difference between male's and female's flexibility is minimal; however, after puberty females are generally more flexible than males. Why? The hormonal differences between males and females is the likely cause of the flexibility differences.[15] Females typically remain more flexible than males throughout their life span.[16] The increased flexibility of females is beneficial during childbirth.

Females are more likely to injure their ACLs than males because of the lesser amount of testosterone in females. "Testosterone strengthens ligaments whereas estrogen weakens ligaments. Other factors that increase the risk of ACL injuries in girls include differences in quadriceps and hamstring

---

[10] Peter Walters and John Byl, *Christian Paths to Health and Wellness*, 3rd ed. (Champaign, IL: Human Kinetics, 2020), 111.

[11] Murray and Kenney, *Practice Guide*, 209.

[12] Hoeger et al., *Lifetime Physical Fitness*, 44–45.

[13] Murray and Kenney, *Practice Guide*, 47.

[14] Murray and Kenney, 168.

[15] Walters and Byl, *Christian Paths to Health and Wellness*, 111.

[16] Hoeger et al., *Lifetime Physical Fitness*, 44–45.

strength as well as differences in the biomechanics of how girls land after jumping."[17]

Females have higher essential body fat (12 percent) than men (3 percent). They have more essential body fat because the fat found in gender-specific areas is included in that percentage.[18] And females need more body fat for their bodies to function than do men.

The differences between males and females are more than hormones. Even the messages sent by culture about how their bodies should look and be shaped are different for males and females. What is the message sent to males? A male should have a "V-shaped, lean and muscular body type."[19] What is the message sent to females? A female *must* be thin and lean, but also curvy in the "right" places. Even the verbiage is different. Males *should* be and females *must* be. Whether it be hormones or cultural messages, males are less likely to suffer from eating disorders than are females. As much as one quarter of those who suffer from eating disorders are males.[20]

More differences between males and females exist that are not included here. What is clear is that males and females are indeed different. Their bodies are different. The messages regarding body image sent to males and females are different. The way they perceive these messages is also different. Science provides overwhelming evidence that males and females are indeed different. A simple way to integrate one's faith into the classroom or even everyday conversation is to point to the lies told by culture regarding the lack of differences in males and females.

Related Scripture

Genesis 1:26–31
Genesis 2:18–25
Psalm 139:13–16
Matthew 6:26
Romans 8:1–11
2 Corinthians 6:14–7:1

---

[17] Murray and Kenney, *Practice Guide*, 21.
[18] Hoeger et al., *Lifetime Physical Fitness*, 21.
[19] Walters and Byl, *Christian Paths to Health and Wellness*, 37.
[20] Murray and Kenney, *Practice Guide*.

Colossians 1:21–23
1 Thessalonians 5:23

<hr>

FURTHER READING

Burns, J. Patout. *Theological Anthropology*. Philadelphia: Fortress, 1981.

Cortez, Marc, and Michael P. Jensen, eds., *T&T Clark Reader in Theological Anthropology*. New York: T&T Clark, 2018.

Cortez, Marc. *Resourcing Theological Anthropology: A Constructive Account of Humanity in the Light of Christ*. Grand Rapids: Zondervan, 2017.

_____. *Theological Anthropology: A Guide for the Perplexed*. New York: T&T Clark, 2010.

Farris, Joshua R. *An Introduction to Theological Anthropology: Humans, Both Creaturely and Divine*. Grand Rapids: Baker, 2020.

Hoekema, Anthony A. *Created in God's Image*. Grand Rapids: Eerdmans, 1986.

Jones, Beth Felker and Jeffrey W. Barbeau, *The Image of God in an Image Driven Age*. Downers Grove: IVP, 2016.

Kilner, John. *Dignity and Destiny: Humanity in the Image of God*. Grand Rapids: Eerdmans, 2015.

Lints, Richard. *Identity and Idolatry: The Image of God and Its Inversion*. Downers Grove, IL: IVP, 2015.

McConville, J. Gordon. *Being Human in God's World: An Old Testament Theology of Humanity*. Grand Rapids: Baker Academic, 2016.

Middleton, J. Richard. *The Liberating Image: The Imago Dei in Genesis 1*. Grand Rapids: Brazos, 2005.

Sherlock, Charles. *The Doctrine of Humanity*. Downers Grove, IL: IVP, 1996.

Strachan, Owen. *Reenchanting Humanity: A Theology of Mankind*. Fearn, UK: Mentor, 2019.

Tennent, Timothy C. *For the Body: Recovering a Theology of Gender, Sexuality, and the Human Body*. Grand Rapids: Zondervan, 2020.

5

Sin

Although we have developed a basic understanding of what it means to be human as created by God, our understanding of human life today falls short if we stop there. While humans were created good by God, and in his image, that goodness was quickly interrupted and his image damaged by the human choice to turn away from God in disobedience and the results of that disobedience. In this brief chapter, we will explore the story of sin and then develop a better grasp on the role that sin plays as a theological category, its impact on what it means to be human, suffering and the type of world that we live in, and the hope that we yearn for in that world.

THE STORY OF SIN

According to the early chapters of Genesis, sin infected creation through Adam and Eve's sin in the garden of Eden. God created Adam and Eve without sin, and he gave them one law: they were not to eat of the Tree of the Knowledge of Good and Evil. Enter the serpent. He tempts Eve by pointing out the appealing qualities of that tree's fruit and calling into question the truth of God's commands: "Did God really say that? Did he really mean it?" Putting Eve in the driver's seat of interpretation, and twisting her desires, the serpent was successful when Eve disobeyed God, ate the fruit, and passed it along to her companion too.

This first sin was no isolated incident but had cascading consequences. Adam and Eve immediately felt changed, enduring shame and hiding from God. Because of their rebellion, God cast them out of the garden of Eden, and the world changed. The consequences included work becoming difficult for Adam and childbirth being painful for Eve. While we might not be able to imagine a reality in which working the ground *is not* difficult or where childbirth *does not* involve pain and danger, the text clearly introduces these as a *result* of sin. Furthermore, the relationship between Adam and Eve became more difficult too. What we see is that sin is no mere personal, internal issue with small consequences. This rebellion changed the human relationship with God, the human relationship with one another, and the human relationship with the created world. When God pronounced these punishments on the first humans in Genesis 3, he also promised to send a deliverer to defeat the enemy, the serpent, who had led them into sin. So, even at the very start, God promised salvation in the midst of sin. He did not deny the consequences, but he did promise a deliverer.

Good readers of Scripture are on the lookout for this deliverer from that point forward in the biblical text. (Part of the reason genealogies are significant is that God promised that a descendant of Eve would be the deliverer; tracing her descendants is important!) What the Old Testament shows us time and again is that this problem of sin not only causes problem after problem, but it impacts and infects even the best and godliest of human leaders that God raises up. We see this with Noah, with Abraham, Isaac, and Jacob, with Moses, with Joshua and the judges, with Saul, David, Solomon, and even the prophets. David, who receives some of the highest praise in the Old Testament as a "man after God's own heart" is also a man who abuses women and kills to get his way. By the end of the Old Testament, it has become clear that no mere human leader can fulfill the promises that God made about sin all the way back in Genesis 3.

Sin and its impact on people reverberate through the rest of Scripture, and Paul gives us one of the clearest reflections on the impact of sin in Romans 5. In verse 12, he explains that sin came into the world through this first sin, and it brought death that has impacted all people. Here we see that Adam and Eve's actions carried consequences for all who came after them. Just as God promised a deliverer in Genesis 3, Paul points to Christ as this deliverer in Romans 5. (But we will get to the details on the doctrine of salvation later.)

THE IMPACT OF SIN AND ITS THEOLOGICAL VOCABULARY

Theological reflection on the reality of sin spans from the biblical text into the theology of the church. In the Old Testament, four concepts expand the notion of sin.[1] First, we see the idea of "crossing the line." Sin involves transgression, crossing a boundary, violating a law. Second, sin carries the notion of "missing the mark." In other words, God has given a good creation, but humans continually fail to live up to whom and what we were created to be. We fall short. Third, sin means rebellion. Sin is conflict with authority and active separation from God. People aren't innocent victims but active rebels, serving idols instead of the true God. Finally, in the Old Testament, sin means death. Sin cuts our relationship with everything: with God, with other people, with the world. It brings death.

The New Testament carries over these same ideas, but it also helps us understand more about the impact of sin. Specifically, we see the relationship between sin and unbelief. As Baptist theologian A. J. Conyers puts it, "Unbelief has not caused sin, and belief has not compensated for sin—rather belief and unbelief is of the very essence of sin."[2] In other words, sin is a manifestation of unbelief; it is not separate from it. Our sin brings us both guilt for breaking God's laws, as well as a sense of shame and humiliation.

Christians have wrestled with how to articulate the nature and origin of human sin according to Scripture. Theologian James Leo Garrett points out two unacceptable approaches that some have taken. First, some believe that sin is due to humanity's finitude or creaturely weakness. This view tends to overemphasize notions like seeing humans as "flesh" (Isa 40:5–8) and misses that creatureliness and finitude are not the root *cause* of sin according to Scripture. As Garrett puts it, "It is *not* that humans are creatures and therefore sinners. Rather, it is that humans are creatures *and* also sinners."[3] Second, others believe that sin is due to bodily desires or instincts. In other words, humans sin because humans have bodies. This view is also based on a misunderstanding of the biblical term "flesh," especially in Romans 7–8 where Paul talks of formerly living "in the flesh" as opposed to "in the spirit." While this view emerged early in the church in relation to certain Greek philosophies and their approach to the body, it has been impacted and morphed in modern times in connection with evolutionary thought. However, all these explanations rely on an understanding of the human that runs in violation of the type of unity between "soul"

---

[1] For more on these, see A. J. Conyers, *A Basic Christian Theology* (Nashville: B&H Academic, 1995), 70ff.
[2] Conyers, 74.
[3] James Leo Garrett Jr., *Systematic Theology*, vol. 1 (Eugene, OR: Wipf & Stock, 2014), 454.

and "body" that we discussed in the previous chapter. The root of sin is not in being physical.

One key term that theologians have used to anchor a proper understanding of the nature and origin of sin is "original sin." This term connects the way the consequences of sin worked out in the Old Testament with the logic found in the New Testament, like that which Paul uses in Romans 5. The term refers to Adam and Eve's sin as "the" original sin, but the term emphasizes Adam's role as our corporate representative, as Paul explains in Romans 5. "Original sin" points to our collective human estrangement from God, from each other, and from creation. Because of original sin, humans inherit a broken human nature from their mothers and fathers. This broken human nature, because of original sin, means that we are all guilty immediately as sinners, and we grow into that reality as we ourselves grow, develop, and choose sin and rebellion. Original sin means we are guilty, and it means we will continue on as sinners if left to our own devices.

Another important term in understanding sin's impact today is "total depravity." While this term is most often associated with Calvinism and a very particular explanation of the way salvation happens, the truth that underlies total depravity is accepted widely by Christians. At root, total depravity means that sin touches and ruins everything about us as humans. In other words, there is no part of us that remains untainted by sin. Any search for a pristine part of the broken human nature, or broken humans, will yield no results. "Total depravity" does not mean that anyone is as bad as he or she can possibly be, or that the world is as bad as it could possibly be. Rather, it points to this important aspect of the doctrine of sin: it has infected us all the way down. We see one hint of this in the Old Testament when the sacrificial system insisted that even unknown sins made people guilty and in need of help (for example, see Leviticus 4). "Total depravity" reminds us that sin infects all that we are, even in ways we are not conscious of. Today, we are most comfortable in thinking of sin as something we set out to do intentionally, knowing we are violating God's laws and rebelling against him. That certainly happens, but sin is more than that! It extends deep within us, beyond what we are conscious of. This truth is also part of what Jesus is getting at when he expounds on the Mosaic law, telling his hearers that the law says murder is wrong, but being angry with someone is too (Matt 5:21–26).

Original sin and total depravity do not mean that all people are aware of their sin. The fact of disagreement about whether sin exists or whether certain things are sinful should come as no surprise. In fact, we see that one of the roles of the Holy Spirit is just that: to convict the unbelieving world of their sin so they might repent and turn to Jesus Christ (John 16:8). Here we see again how the different doctrines connect and overlap. We'll discuss more on the Holy Spirit in a later chapter.

SIN AND SUFFERING

What is the relationship between sin and suffering? What about the brokenness of the world? One of the most difficult pieces to understand in relation to sin and the doctrine of God is God's relationship to sin and the evil that follows from sin. Typically, Christians have talked about two types of evil resulting from sin: moral evil and natural evil. Moral evil includes consequences of actions that are directly sinful and evil: murder, for instance. Natural evil refers to the way the warped and broken world causes pain and suffering among humans. Think hurricanes or floods. According to Scripture, creation itself is broken, waiting "with groans" for salvation to be completely accomplished (Rom 8:19–23). Both forms of evil result from sin.

But what is God's role here? Scripture nowhere shows God directly doing evil. Early biblical narratives point this out right away. In the story of Joseph, his brothers clearly intend evil. They sell him into slavery for their own benefit and his harm. Yet God is at work, using even their evil, sinful choices to work out his plan to keep Joseph's family safe. As Joseph reflects late in his life, what the brothers intended for evil, God intended for good (Gen 50:20). In the book of Exodus, we witness a dance of sorts between Pharaoh and God. The idea of Pharaoh's "hardened heart" points to the way that his sin impacted his heart to drive him to more sin and rebellion against the true God. The text tells us vaguely that "Pharaoh's heart was hard" (Exod 7:22) but also that Pharaoh "hardened his heart" (Exod 8:15). But we also see that God "hardened Pharaoh's heart" (Exod 9:12). Here we see God orienting evil to his purposes, redeeming evil intentions into a greater story. While the Bible always shows God as sovereign and in control, he is not the author of sin or the one tempting people to sin (Jas 1:13). Humans choose to sin. But part of the hope God provides is that he can use even our worst choices to bring about and fulfill his great promises of salvation.

CONCLUSION

Christians certainly explain sin in different ways and disagree on its exact impact on how humans live. In the early church, one teacher named Pelagius attempted to reformulate the way Christians thought about sin. Pelagius believed that God would not command people to do something that they could not do, so if God commanded people to be holy, it must be possible for them to be holy under their own power. Sin might have an influence, but it could not be too large of one. The theologian Augustine vehemently disagreed, arguing for a deeper view of sin, one that acknowledged—as Scripture does—that humans are dead in our trespasses and sins, not merely confused (Eph 2:1). Early Christians recognized Augustine's version as the one to be faithfully drawing on Scripture. Christians continue to disagree on where exactly grace begins to root out sin, and how that impacts human choice, repentance, and faith. We will turn to that in a later chapter. But Christians agree that the sin of Adam and Eve has infected all humanity, leading to a problem that no mere human can solve independently. Our doctrine of humanity reminds us that we were created for communion with God. The doctrine of sin explains how we have broken this relationship, and how we must rely on God to fix it.

Sociology and the Doctrine of Sin
MATT HENDERSON

Since its inception as a discipline, sociology in the United States has been guided by at least two important impulses. The first is an impulse to view human events through a teleological lens; that is, to explain human outcomes as resulting from impersonal transhistorical processes, rather than from human choices. As influential scholar William Sewell Jr. notes, the most famous early theorists, such as Comte, Marx, and Durkheim, tended to view history as an inexorable progression of events toward a natural end, and the tendency to assume that history continues to move on a forward trajectory, continues to animate contemporary scholarship.[4]

The second impulse holds that the ultimate purpose of social inquiry is to make the world more just and equitable. Since its formal establishment during the Progressive Era, American Sociology has always maintained a spirit of social reform coherent with the moral assumptions of its age. For example, one key figure in developing some of the initial practices of sociology (and of social workers) was Jane Addams. Addams was both a prominent social reformer and an adherent of the Social Gospel, a movement that explicitly advocated and organized collective efforts to address multiple social ills, including poverty, poor housing, prostitution, etc. Like other Social Gospel adherents, Addams's efforts were at least partly motivated by her Christian convictions. Similarly, contemporary sociologists maintain a deep interest in advocating social reform aimed at decreasing wealth inequality, improving the material conditions of the poor, and advocating for the interests of the socially marginalized. And although the field is now largely secular, the manner which many sociologists commit to improving conditions for the "poor and marginalized" can appear to take on a quasi-religious character in practice.

Though distinct, these impulses are usually harmonious. Sociology as practiced in the United States appears to syncretize a value for making the world a better place, usually by radically altering large social structures and institutions, while assuming human progress to be irresistible, and that their efforts are fated to produce holistic good.

Naturally, there is significant overlap between these two impulses and a Christian worldview. Christian eschatology holds that all human history unfolds toward Jesus's ultimate redeeming of creation. Christianity also teaches us to care for the poor and marginalized. So, at first blush, it might be difficult to see anything objectionable about these twin impulses. But the doctrine of sin invites us to examine them more closely. While there is much more to be said in what follows, I will emphasize how sin teaches that our efforts are insufficient for redeeming creation. It is only through Jesus, and in our obedience to him, that we participate in God's redeeming

---

[4] William H. Sewell, *Logics of History: Social Theory and Social Transformation* (Chicago: University of Chicago Press, 2005).

of the world. Despite how clever we are, how effectively we organize, how pure our motives, how well intended our plans, or even how successfully we achieve our goals, all human effort has fallen, and will continue to fall short of redeeming the world.

Therefore, the doctrine of sin condemns these twin impulses of hubris. The successes of the Social Gospel movement are instructive, here. Probably the movement's greatest legislative victory was the passage of the Eighteenth Amendment and the prohibition of alcohol. This represented a major social reform promising to reduce rates of alcoholism, spousal abuse, and absentee parenting, and contribute to the overall health of the nation. Instead, the new law spawned many unintended and pernicious outcomes, such as increased alcoholism and violent crime in urban centers, decreased trust in the rule of law, increased sexual promiscuity, and a decline in federal tax revenue, revenue which could have been useful to enterprising social reformers. The amendment was famously repealed.

What I find instructive about this example is not whether the actions of reformers were justifiable or foolhardy—in fact, I think they are quite defensible, given the high rates of alcoholism in the nineteenth and early twentieth centuries, and the social dysfunction associated with them. Rather, it was that their efforts produced outcomes that could have hardly been anticipated, despite how glaring they might appear in hindsight. What also stands out are the unanticipated ways human wickedness adjusted to its new human constraints.

I do not mean to say that social reform is doomed to total failure, and there are plenty of examples of social reform worthy of praise. Rather, the doctrine of sin reminds us that no human institution can exist without human frailty, and that frailty undermines even our noblest attempts to create a better world. History is littered with so many cases of well-intentioned efforts to produce a good society, which only contributed to barbarism and chaos. Taking the doctrine of sin seriously provokes us to consider not just our own wickedness and frailty, but the wickedness and frailty of even our best institutions.

While sociology might tend to overlook human frailty, its insights can be very illuminating for American Christians who struggle to understand the consequences of sin beyond their own behavior. Often, when students of mine are confronted with how much social inequality and disorder there is in the world, they reflexively question how these problems might be ameliorated with social policy or by radically altering social order. They wonder how we might be able to apply reason and ingenuity so that these problems might be "solved." In this respect, the students at our small Christian college reflect the orthodoxy of most Americans, and of sociology for that matter. Few of them ask questions about how the church should bear witness to these realities. Seldom do they ask about the church's lamentable role in exacerbating these problems. Seldom do they reflect about the limits of human intervention but the limitlessness of God's sovereignty. Seldom do they lament and repent of their own participation in our fallen world. Rather, their reflex is one of defensiveness—that the world isn't that bad, nor are they especially culpable for it—or of despair—that there is no solution for our fallen world.

This response is one I think many American Christians, especially evangelicals, are prone to have when they are confronted with the totality of social disorder. To address this, I offer the following critique: many churches in America proffer insufficient teaching about sin, leaving many American Christians with an insufficient theological grasp of sin and its consequences. In the evangelical world I grew up in, sin was typically described as a matter of individual piety. It was the thing that kept you out of heaven. It was a list of behaviors one should or should not do.

This is all true, but incomplete. This way of teaching about sin fails to describe how human depravity, faithlessness, fear, and greed infect and corrupt social institutions. It fails to explain the fallen nature of governments, cultures, and economies. It also inflames the oblique heresy common in American Christianity: that individual piety is the remedy for all social problems. Of course, individual piety is a crucial part of our discipleship; but the Bible is quite clear about its insufficiency as a remedy for sin (Heb 7:19). Rather, God's solution for social disorder is the same one for individual disorder: the church. Jesus points to the church, the edified body of Christ, imbued by the Holy Spirit, as the solution to a fallen world.

Sociology is of tremendous instructional value here because it demonstrates how corporate, complex, and comprehensive sin is in characterizing every aspect of social life—how deeply it imbues the world. We can see how violent, chaotic, and grotesque the world becomes when we lean on our own understanding. When we consider how complicated and inexorably fallen our world is, we grow a deeper reverence for the cross and are drawn closer to his church, as a place where we can lament of the fallen nature of our world, where we can repent of our role in it, and where we can be edified to not only sin less, but rejoice at the ongoing work of redemption the Lord has enlisted us to participate in.

Related Scripture

Genesis 3
Psalm 51
Matthew 5:21–48
Romans 1:18–32
Romans 3:10–18
Romans 3:23
Romans 5:12–21
Romans 6:23
Romans 7:7–25
James 1:12–15
James 2:8–13

FURTHER READING

Harmon, Matthew S. *Rebels and Exiles: A Biblical Theology of Sin and Restoration*. Downers Grove, IL: IVP Academic, 2020.

McCall, Thomas H. *Against God and Nature: The Doctrine of Sin*. Wheaton, IL: Crossway, 2019.

Morgan, Christopher, and Robert Peterson, eds. *Fallen: A Theology of Sin*. Wheaton, IL: Crossway, 2013.

Plantinga, Cornelius Jr. *Not the Way It's Supposed to Be: A Breviary of Sin*. Grand Rapids: Eerdmans, 1996.

Poe, Harry Lee. *See No Evil: The Existence of Sin in an Age of Relativism*. Grand Rapids: Kregel, 2004.

Smith, David L. *With Willful Intent: A Theology of Sin*. Grand Rapids: Baker, 1994.

Stump, J. B., and Chad Meister. *Original Sin and the Fall: Five Views*. Downers Grove, IL: IVP Academic, 2020.

6

Person of Christ

M any Christians take knowing Jesus for granted. Evangelicals, for instance, emphasize that each person needs to come into a saving, personal relationship with the Savior. Often, when I begin talking about the doctrine of Christ in class, I tell students that I suspect most of them lean toward heresy in their thinking about Jesus. You might as well; I know I do. Do you think of Jesus primarily as God, or primarily as human? Which one is easier? In this chapter, we will explore the doctrine of the person of Christ: the incarnation of the Second Person of the Trinity, the distinction between his divine and human natures, and the unity of the one person, Jesus Christ. Hopefully, through paying careful attention to what Scripture reveals, and refusing the all-too-easy simplifications, we will move a little closer to a proper understanding of Jesus Christ.

Theologians typically divide the doctrine of Christology into the person of Christ and the work of Christ. Obviously, these relate. Understanding the work of Christ gives us clues to who he is, but we must understand something about who Jesus is for us to interpret properly what his life and death mean, and especially what his death on the cross means. And we must understand the cross to understand salvation.

For the early church, the possibility of salvation hinged on getting this doctrine right. For the early theologian Athanasius, only God could save people from sin. Christians believed that Jesus saves people from sin. Therefore, Jesus must be fully God. And as another early leader, Gregory of Nazianzus put it, "What is not assumed, is not redeemed."[1] In other words, if Jesus Christ was not fully and completely human, then he could not offer salvation to humans. Through their preaching, letters, and councils, early church leaders insisted on

---

[1] This common quotation comes from Gregory's letter to Cledonius, Epistle 101.

the full humanity of Jesus and the full divinity of Jesus. These were not esoteric debates; the logic of salvation depended on it.

Today, the world finds it hard to believe—or, frankly, ridiculous to believe—that Jesus is God. But for early Christians, there was just as much pushback from their contemporaries that Jesus could not have been human. In other words, some systems of belief were more ready to take Jesus on as a divine figure of some sort, but they were unwilling to acknowledge his full humanity. We will begin there, and even if you tend to take the humanity of Jesus for granted, it is important to understand why early Christians insisted on this aspect of the doctrine of Christology.

HUMANITY OF JESUS

Jesus's full humanity is demonstrated throughout the Gospels. He had a fully human body (born of a woman) and lived a fully human life. We see that Jesus "increased in wisdom" (Luke 2:52) and was subject to the same physiological limitations that we are: he got hungry (Matt 4:2), thirsty (John 19:28), and tired (John 4:6). He suffered and died. He suffered when he was beaten, when the crown of thorns was pressed into his head, when he was nailed to the cross, and as he died (Mark 15). Jesus *looked* human; his contemporaries had a genuine physical perception of him. We are reminded of this in 1 John 1:1–3:

> What was from the beginning, what we have heard, what we have seen with our eyes, what we have observed and have touched with our hands, concerning the word of life—that life was revealed, and we have seen it and we testify and declare to you the eternal life that was with the Father and was revealed to us—what we have seen and heard we also declare to you, so that you may also have fellowship with us; and indeed our fellowship is with the Father and with his Son, Jesus Christ.

Jesus as we see him in the Gospels is human physiologically.

But should this lead us to think of Jesus as "human on the outside, divine on the inside"? Sometimes we are tempted to follow this heresy because it makes sense to us. But the Gospels show Jesus having a human "interior life" as well. He thought, reasoned, and felt emotion. He was moved by human situations—he marveled at the faith of the centurion (Luke 7:9) and wept at the death of Lazarus (John 11:35). He was troubled before his crucifixion (Matt 26:37). In the words of Millard Erickson, "He did everything they did, except sin and pray for forgiveness. He ate with them, he bled, he slept, he cried. If Jesus was not human, then surely no one ever has been."[2] This statement means that Jesus is human spiritually as well as physiologically. He has a human nature and everything that nature entails: a body, a soul, a spirit.

Two early heresies rejected this part of the doctrine of Christ. The Docetists argued that Jesus was *not* human; rather, he was something like a very convincing ghost. He only appeared to be human. Later, Apollinarianism argued that Jesus had a partial humanity. He had a human body, but he lacked a human soul (or whatever term you want to use for the interior experience of the human). In class, I often call this the "God in a bod" heresy: Jesus was the spiritual second person stuck inside a human body. The early Christians rejected this, because it meant that Jesus was not fully human, and it also did not line up with the way the Gospels speak of Jesus. If Jesus was going to redeem all of humanity, he had to take on full humanity, body and soul. But if Jesus is fully human, in body and soul, what is left over to be divine? We will look next at the divinity of Jesus before turning to how we can understand both of these natures together in one person.

DIVINITY OF JESUS

The New Testament speaks with one voice that Jesus is God. We see it everywhere. In Jesus's own life, he demonstrates that he thought of himself as God. He claimed he had authority over God's stipulations about the Sabbath (Mark 2:27–28) and that he could command angels (Matt 13:41), forgive sins (Mark 2:5), and give life (John 5:21). He claimed unity with God the Father (John 10:30; 14:7–9), and in his trial he used language about himself that was clearly Messianic and exalted (Matt 26:63–64). He had a habit of putting his own words right alongside the Word of God in the Old Testament (see the pattern through the Sermon on the Mount in Matt 5–7), he used titles like "Son of God," and he allowed people to call him God (Thomas's confession in John

---

[2] Erickson, *Introducing Christian Doctrine*, 251, (see chap. 1, n. 2).

20:28). As C. S. Lewis famously put it, Jesus was either a liar, a lunatic, or the Lord.[3]

These divine claims don't stop in the Gospels. For instance, the book of Hebrews begins:

> Long ago God spoke to our ancestors by the prophets at differ-
> ent times and in different ways. In these last days, he has spoken
> to us by his Son. God has appointed him heir of all things and
> made the universe through him. The Son is the radiance of
> God's glory and the exact expression of his nature, sustaining
> all things by his powerful word. After making purification for
> sins, he sat down at the right hand of the Majesty on high. So
> he became superior to the angels, just as the name he inherited
> is more excellent than theirs. (1:1–4)

What exalted language! Radiance of God's glory; exact expression of his nature. Paul uses similar language. Jesus is the image of the invisible God, and all things hold together in him (Col 1:15–20). He uses similar terms in Phil 2:5–11. For these things to be true consistently requires Jesus to be fully God.

Two early heresies rejected this idea and proposed others. For the Ebionites, Jesus was just an ordinary man with extraordinary gifts of righteousness and wisdom. For Arians, Jesus was the first and highest created being, but not divine in the same sense as God the Father. The church carefully rejected both ways of thinking as pastors over time developed clearer ways of holding together the various claims of Scripture in relation to Jesus and the doctrine of the Trinity.

Jesus's divinity means that when we see Jesus, we see God (John 14:9). We can (and should) worship Jesus. His divinity makes salvation possible, because his sacrificial death was not only the death of a mere human. And his divinity, when considered with his humanity, gives us an amazing picture of the fact that the divine and the human do not have to exist in conflict or competition; rather, God and humanity are reunited, both in Christ's person and in his work. Let's turn to this idea of holding these two natures together.

---

[3] C. S. Lewis, *Mere Christianity* (New York: HarperCollins, 2001), 52. In other editions, see bk. 2, chap. 3.

ONE JESUS: THE HYPOSTATIC UNION

The easiest way to conceive of Jesus's full humanity and his full divinity is to imagine two people, sometimes-comfortably but sometimes-uncomfortably sharing a body. A new day dawns, Jesus's body is still tired, and an interior dialogue ensues:

Human Jesus: "I'd like five more minutes."

Divine Jesus: "Nope, let's go. Up. I've been waiting long enough while you sleep."

Human Jesus: "Come on, you're always acting better than me."

This brief, fake dialogue is obvious enough to help us see the error. Of course, we do not really think of Jesus having dueling persons inside his body. But do we think this way sometimes when we read and interpret the Gospels? When we slow down and think about it, the Bible always treats Jesus as one person. There is never a scene like the one above, with two agents in Jesus's thoughts or actions. Jesus always spoke in the singular: "I and the Father are one" (John 10:30). Others did the same thing: Paul stated that Jesus was "manifested in the flesh, vindicated in the Spirit, seen by angels, preached among the nations, . . . [and] taken up in glory" (1 Tim 3:16). He did not say, "Human Jesus was in the flesh; Divine Jesus was who our preaching is really about and who went up in glory." No—there is one Jesus, with all these true aspects.

How are we supposed to understand Jesus's two natures?

Let us begin by understanding various missteps that answers have taken. We will look briefly at three. First, Nestorianism simplified the issue by rejecting unity, the idea that the two natures were united in one person. Instead, Nestorianism eventually morphed to the implication that there were effectively two unique persons operating within the one Jesus, a human person and a divine one. Second, Eutychianism simplified the issue by rejecting the two natures, instead arguing that the human nature and the divine nature combined in such a way that a third, hybrid nature resulted. Jesus did not exactly have a human nature, and he did not exactly have a divine nature. Instead, these two natures mixed to create one divine-human nature, which brought together elements of both. In effect, the aspects of the divine nature sort of overwhelm the human nature in this new hybrid nature. In the end, Jesus is not quite human OR quite divine. Third, adoptionism simplified the issue by eliminating the divine nature from consideration as a real nature that Jesus had. Instead, Jesus was a remarkable human man that God chose to adopt and make "divine" by association. In a key way, this is the exact opposite of what Scripture presents. In adoptionism we have a human becoming divine. As we will explore momentarily, Scripture presents us with God becoming human without ceasing to be God.

Two big terms help us understand the picture that God provides in Scripture: *hypostatic union* and *the communication of attributes.*

First, the term "hypostatic union" serves to balance the duality of natures and the unity of the person of Jesus Christ. In other words, Jesus has two natures, and he is one person. How are the two natures united? They are united in the one person, Jesus. Hence the "hypostatic" (personal) union. When we speak of "nature" here, we are dealing with a complicated idea, but one we can simplify for our purposes. (Like much in this book, entire monographs have been written on this if you are interested in more detailed exploration.) I usually tell students to begin to think of a nature as made up of "things"—loosely defined—that we would put on a list that make something what it is. The divine nature, then, would be the list of things that make God, God. The human nature would be the list of things that make humans, human. (I am working with an understanding that there is something substantive to what it means to be human, as we explored in the chapter on the doctrine of humanity. Modern people who see "human" as a malleable term would reject this notion of natures, entirely.) When we confess in faith that Jesus has two natures, we mean that he has everything on both lists. The term "person" is likewise complicated, but in a beginning exploration like this one we can be satisfied with something like a conscious acting agent. Jesus only has one of these; he is one person. The hypostatic union, then, explains that these two natures only come together in the one person who is Jesus Christ.

When we consider the hypostatic union, there are two approaches that can help us make some sense of it. First, follow the shape of the biblical narrative in your understanding of this idea. There is and always has been this eternally existing Second Person of the Trinity, the Son, who has eternally had possession of the divine nature by virtue of being, well, the eternally existing Second Person of the Trinity. That Person, at the right time, is sent by the Father in the power of the Spirit to take on flesh—not "put on flesh" as though it were a suit, but "put on flesh" in the sense of "take on everything that it means to be human" (see John 1:14). Following this narrative helps because it reminds us that we are not taking one part divinity, one part humanity, and shaking them up to create something new. No, God has always existed as Trinity. The Second Person has not always been human, but once the Father sent him to take on flesh (the incarnation), he has been and always will be human. There is not a new or additional person involved; he is the same person. He takes on human nature in a way that does not change his divine nature—or, what it means to be God.

The second way that we can make some sense of the hypostatic union is to start with the person as we see him: Jesus of Nazareth. In other words, we do not begin by thinking of some abstraction of "what it means to be God" and then some abstraction of "what it means to be human" and then try to imagine what sort of being might be able to combine those two abstractions. Rather, we start by looking at the face of the Savior, at Jesus Christ in his life, death, burial, and resurrection. It is there, looking at Christ, that we see the clearest picture of God ("Immanuel," God with us) as well as the clearest picture of what it means to be human (after all, Jesus had a human nature, but not a fallen, sinful human nature). The Son is not more or less God than the Father, but the Son is the one who took on flesh and walked among us. (When Jesus makes statements such as "The Father is greater than I" [John 14:28], he is speaking of himself as a man.) And the Son does become more fully human than we have been able to experience so far, because he embodies perfect humanity rather than the fallen and partial humanity that we experience and endure in our lives. Christ not only dies for us on the cross, he demonstrates in his life that the divine nature and the human nature are not necessarily in conflict, but only in conflict because of sin.

At this point we can turn again to Millard Erickson's words: "If Jesus was not human, then surely no one ever has been."[4]

Could Jesus sin? This is a helpful question that the second "big" term will help us explore: "the doctrine of the communication of attributes."

The basic idea of the communication of attributes is that anything that is true of one of Jesus's two natures is true of Jesus's person. The attributes of the individual nature are "communicated," or can be said to be true, of his person. This doctrine saves us from one easy mistake when we think about Jesus: we should not think that Jesus's human nature died on the cross, as though that would mean that Jesus's person did not in fact die. No, Jesus died on the

---

[4] Erickson, *Introducing Christian Doctrine*, 251.

cross. The communication of attributes reminds us that persons do things; natures make things possible or potential. Natures are not out there operating independently. We might say that persons "animate" natures, but that has its limitations as well. The idea is that natures do not do things; people do. So, on the cross, Jesus died. Human natures do not die. Divine natures do not die. People die. Jesus died on the cross.

This idea also helps us better understand the question of Jesus and sin. We must do some sorting out here, first of all. As we learned earlier in the doctrine of humanity, Adam and Eve were created with human natures that made it possible for them to sin or not to sin. By their choosing to sin, they infected their descendants with fallen human natures, which make it impossible for us not to sin. Jesus, however, in taking on flesh, took on a perfect human nature, not a sinful human nature. But it is still possible for a person with a human nature to sin (it is certain that a person with a fallen human nature will sin). Christians differ here on exactly how to parse out these details. However, one way of putting it together is to say that it was hypothetically possible for Jesus to sin, because the quality of "possible to sin" can be communicated from his nature to his person. But because this person is the divine person, the eternal Logos, Holy God himself, it is really no possibility at all. This is because at the same time, the divine nature includes the impossibility of sin. That, too, must be communicated to his person. This leads us to the point where we can provide something of an answer: Jesus, by virtue of having a human nature, had the possibility and opportunity to sin, but because he also has a fully divine nature, he had the certainty that he would always think, feel, and act for the glory of God. We know from Scripture that Jesus was without sin (2 Cor 5:21), and this framework of the communication of attributes helps us better understand how that makes sense even with Jesus having a fully human nature.

CONCLUSION

As I mentioned at the start of this chapter, theologians typically talk about the person and work of Christ separately, and we will do that here, focusing on the work in the next chapter. But we must be careful not to unnecessarily divide these two. As we have seen, Jesus's work, and especially his resurrection, are key pieces of "data" that we must consider in coming to understand who Jesus is. On the other side, the only way that we can properly interpret the work of Jesus is to remind ourselves continually that this is the fully God, fully human, Jesus Christ who is doing these works. Without that, we will misunderstand them too. As with all of theology, there is a somewhat logical way to talk about the different doctrines and topics, but they are always intertwined and mutually reinforcing.

Philosophy and the Person of Christ
ROSS PARKER

How does the doctrine of the person of Christ challenge particular issues, practices, or assumptions in your field of study?

Philosophy is notoriously hard to define; what falls under the discipline of philosophy is difficult to demarcate. But there are questions that clearly fall under the discipline of philosophy. One fundamental area of philosophy is *epistemology*, which is the study of knowledge and reasonable belief. Another area of philosophy concerns fundamental questions about humanity—we can refer to this as *philosophical anthropology*.

There is a strand of philosophical reflection that claims that what we can claim to know is that which we can reasonably believe based on reason and common human experience. (This is an oversimplification, but I think it reflects an approach to knowledge held by many.) If we adopt this approach to knowledge, it will lead to what might seem like reasonable conclusions about the nature of humans. For example, are humans capable of being morally perfect? Well, if we go with the data of our experience, even if that experience is wide-ranging, we will probably draw the conclusion that no human is capable of being morally perfect (have you ever met anyone who is even close?). One plausible explanation for that is that humans by nature *can't* be morally perfect. As Alexander Pope said, "to err is human . . ."

But the Christian teaching on the person of Christ tells us that Jesus is fully human, and it also teaches us that Jesus is morally perfect. This has at least two implications.

One implication concerns philosophical anthropology—our approach to understanding what it means to be human. Contrary to the broadly empirical approach mentioned earlier, we should not form our understanding of human nature based on experience of people around us, even if that experience is varied. Our understanding of what it means to be human should take into account the incarnation. Christian doctrine tells us that we can understand what it is to be human *most fully* in the person of Jesus.

A second implication concerns our understanding of sources of epistemic justification and knowledge. If Christianity is true, then our methods for coming to know about reality should not be limited to what we can know based on reason and common human experience. We should also consider the content of special revelation—information that we could not come to on our own, that we are given by God—in forming our understanding of humanity, and more broadly in forming our understanding of all aspects of reality.

How does your field of study provide a unique perspective or way of thinking that can help Christians better understand this doctrine or related topics?

There are some philosophers (certainly not all, but some) who think that religious people are unconcerned with their beliefs being logically coherent and consistent. And unfortunately, there are some Christians who reinforce this view of religious belief. Looking at the history of Christian reflection on the doctrine of the person of Christ, however, should make clear that most Christians throughout the centuries have emphasized the need to formulate our understanding of the person of Christ in such a way that we do *not* affirm something contradictory about Christ. The truth about the person of Christ will exceed our comprehensive grasp, but the doctrine will not be contradictory.

This is an area where philosophy serves as a handmaid to theology. Again, philosophy is a difficult discipline to define, but a commonly understood methodological commitment of philosophy is carefully defining terms and making distinctions. Many people have understood what Christians teach about the person of Christ to be contradictory. To take just one alleged contradiction—Christians affirm that the Father is God, and that the Son (Jesus) is God, and that the Holy Spirit is God, and that the Father and the

Son and the Holy Spirit are distinct, and yet there is one God. Don't these affirmations imply that there is one God *and* there are three Gods? But as Aristotle put it, "Nothing can both be and not be at the same time and in the same respect." Christians do not affirm that God is one and God is three in *the same respect*. What is affirmed is that God is one in essence (nature), and God is three in person. So there's not a blatant contradiction when we carefully make distinctions, which is something that philosophy focuses on.

Related Scripture

Matthew 1:18–28
Luke 2:40–52
John 1:1–34
John 6:35; 8:12–38; 10:7; 11:25; 10:11; 14:6; 15:1
Philippians 2:1–11
Colossians 1:15–23
Hebrews 4:14–5:10

FURTHER READING

Cole, Graham. *The God Who Became Human: A Biblical Theology of Incarnation*. Downers Grove, IL: IVP Academic, 2013.

Letham, Robert. *The Message of the Person of Christ*. Downers Grove, IL: IVP Academic, 2013.

Macleod, Donald. *The Person of Christ*. Downers Grove, IL: IVP, 1998.

Wellum, Stephen. *God the Son Incarnate: The Doctrine of Christ*. Wheaton, IL: Crossway, 2016.

_____. *The Person of Christ: An Introduction*. Wheaton, IL: Crossway, 2021.

Wright, N. T. *The Challenge of Jesus: Rediscovering Who Jesus Was and Is*. Downers Grove, IL: IVP, 1999.

7

Work of Christ

As noted in the previous chapter, there is a bit of necessary circularity between the questions of the person and the work of Christ. To understand properly who Jesus is, we must understand what he has done. But to understand what he has done, we must understand who he is, fully human and fully God. We began where most theologians do, exploring the person of Christ in the last chapter. With that under our belt, we will turn to the work of Christ. Historically, Christians have found it helpful to talk about the work of Christ using three "offices." That is a strange term for us—in the academic world, especially, we think of offices as rooms (hopefully though not always) with windows and bookshelves. Here we are using "office" in the sense of an official position, usually of authority. Each of these three offices are introduced in the Old Testament. When we reflect on these three offices, we see Jesus as the perfect fulfillment of what the Old Testament was gesturing toward in these offices, and the offices themselves help us better understand all of what Jesus came to do rather than only emphasizing one particular aspect to the neglect of others.

THE OFFICES: PROPHET, PRIEST, KING

The first office that Jesus fulfills is that of prophet. Starting here is important for a few reasons. First, for many of us, "the work of Christ" makes us think immediately of the work that Jesus performed on the cross. On the one hand, that is not a problem at all! Jesus himself said that he came to give his life as a ransom for many (Mark 10:45), and if Jesus is happy to define the purpose of his life that way, we should be too! On the other hand, if we jump immediately to Jesus's work on the cross, we can misunderstand what he did the rest of the time he was on earth. We might tend to think he was basically waiting around, doing some carpentry as a hobby, and then finally deciding to run around for a few years with a crew of disciples just for fun. We of course would not say it that way, but sometimes we treat the life of Christ that way!

Jesus fulfills the role of *prophet*, first, because he is the ultimate communicator of God's Truth to the world. He reveals God. He does this, of course, because he IS God. Additionally, the Second Person of the Trinity is revealed to us in places like John 1 using the idea of the *"logos"* or "the word." Jesus's incarnation is a taking-on-flesh of the Eternal Word.

Not only is Jesus the Eternal Word, but he also undertakes a ministry of teaching and preaching that also fulfills this prophetic office. Again, Jesus did not take up teaching to fill time until the crucifixion. Jesus spoke God's Word with great authority, an authority that drew people to him to better understand the kingdom of God and its message. Jesus is of course more than a prophet, but his teaching ministry is meant to tell us true things about what the kingdom of God is like, and how his followers should act within it. And, here in the prophetic role, we see another place where Jesus's death and resurrection are significant: Jesus himself predicted them (Matt 17:22–23), and as the Old Testament teaches, prophets are confirmed when their predictions come true and rejected when they do not (Deut 18:22). This poses a problem for anyone who wants to accept Jesus as a teacher but not a Savior: Jesus said he would be killed and raised. If he indeed did that, he is nothing less than the Savior of the World. If he did not do that, then he was at best a failed (and therefore deceptive) prophet. There is no middle ground, even when focusing only on Jesus as the Great Prophet.

Second, Jesus fulfills the role of *priest*. Many Christians think about this role the most when they think about the work Jesus came to do, because they think of Jesus primarily as coming to die on the cross. I do not want to downplay the centrality of the cross at all, but we also must make sure we do not reduce the work of Christ only to its central element. Jesus fulfills the role of priest by making himself the ultimate sacrifice that reconciles sinful humans with God. Jesus's work on the cross is central to his earthly mission and work. As noted above, Jesus himself said it was the purpose for his incarnation. We will return to a fuller discussion of Jesus's work on the cross in the next section of this chapter.

We should not limit his priestly work to the cross, however. Jesus also exercises the priestly office during his earthly ministry. He proclaims the forgiveness of sins—something that the priests in the Old Testament did in conjunction with the sacrificial system. And this move was not lost on Jesus's enemies, who pointed out the seeming problem of promising forgiveness in this way (Luke 7:48). Not only did Jesus forgive sins; he also healed people. In the Old Testament, the priests were responsible for dealing with infectious skin diseases (Leviticus 13) and even mold problems in homes (Lev 14:33–53). While we do not see Jesus as a home inspector in the Gospels, we certainly see him healing. This healing points to his divine nature, and it also says something about the coming kingdom of God, where there will be no tears or suffering (Rev 21:4). But it also connects to the priestly office. Finally, we see Jesus's priestly work in his simple act of praying for his followers. In John 14–16, Jesus prays for his disciples, and he even prays for us directly, asking God's grace on those who would come to believe through the apostles' teaching (John 20:29). In the book of Hebrews, Jesus is lifted up as the ultimate high priest because of his sacrifice, but also because of his work of intercession, praying for us and pleading for us.

Third, Jesus fulfills the office of *king*. We see this in the rule of Christ, who reigns over the universe (Matt 28:18). This reign, of course, is something that we catch glimpses of now but will see fully in the future. But Jesus even now holds the universe together (Colossians 1), and his disciples clearly picked up that they were in the presence of a great king, stooping to argue about future court positions during their travels (Luke 9:46). The disciples had some basic misunderstandings about Jesus as king, but they were mistakes of underestimation: they thought he might kick out the Romans and rule over geographical Israel. Their problem was not in thinking that Jesus was a king; their problem was in underestimating the extent of his rule and completely missing the means by which he would bring in his kingdom (again, reminding us of the centrality of the cross).

Each office reveals something important about Jesus's work. The prophetic role reminds us that Jesus teaching ministry was not just filling up time while waiting for crucifixion. Jesus is God's Word, proclaims God's Word, and expects his disciples to follow his teaching. The priestly role helps us see not only the centrality of the cross and Jesus's sacrifice, but also the way that his healings and prayers fit in. Last, the office of king reminds us that in this first-century Jewish rabbi figure we also have the One who holds all things together—at the name of whom every knee will bow and tongue confess, because of his conquering death.

THE CROSS AND ATONEMENT

When we ask the question, "What did Jesus accomplish on the cross?" we are primarily addressing his role as priest, but the other two roles are present as well. For instance, the cross proclaims something about the problem of sin and its solution, through the very act of the Son of God confronting death. The prophetic role is there. In addition, Jesus's crucifixion involved soldiers mocking his kingly role: pressing a crown of thorns on his head and ridiculing him with a sign over the cross. The resurrection vindicates Jesus in his fulfillment of the office of king. Again, limiting Jesus's work to his priestly role can make such aspects invisible to us. Still, the priestly role is central on the cross, and it in fact empowers and enlivens these other offices. The prophetic proclamation of the cross is rooted in the sacrifice Jesus makes as priest, and he accomplishes victory over sin, demonstrating his kingship, through sacrifice as well.

As we focus on the cross, we are focusing on the doctrine of the atonement. "Atonement" is one of the few technical theological terms rooted in the English language. The ideas are certainly present in theological literature from the earliest days of the church, but the word "atonement" that we use today derives from an English etymology, basically "at-one-ment," highlighting that the doctrine is about taking two alienated parties and making them one. It unifies them, reconciling them together.

The atonement is rooted in what God revealed about sin and reconciliation in the Old Testament. The entire sacrificial system points to and develops this idea that sin requires the shedding of blood. Jesus clearly understood himself and his sacrifice in connection with this system (Matt 20:28; Mark 10:45; John 13:1–17), as do the other New Testament writers. It isn't as though God the Father didn't know what to do about sin before sending Jesus, so he simply invented a sacrificial system to keep the Jews busy until the Son took on flesh. Rather, the sacrificial system was meant to prepare God's people for the ultimate sacrifice of Jesus, demonstrating the significance of sin as well as the limitations of other sacrifices. We see this especially in the book of Hebrews, which develops this idea of Jesus as the Great High Priest who fulfills the Old Testament sacrificial system (Heb 4:14–16).

What does this matter for us today, who do not practice the sacrificial system? We can see why it would be important for ancient Jews to see the connections of Jesus to this system, but what about us? To comprehend what Jesus did on the cross, we must understand it within this trajectory of God's revelation about sin and the possibility of reconciliation. If we do not take seriously the sacrificial system and Jesus's fulfillment of it, we will miss some of what is happening on the cross and be tempted to reduce it to categories that make more sense to us: simply a demonstration of love, or perhaps a necessary way to identify with the oppressed. The cross surely demonstrates love, and Jesus certainly is oppressed by Rome. But those are important descriptions only in connection with the sacrificial system's fulfillment. Jesus's fulfillment of the system is truly a fulfillment, a better sacrifice that makes repeated sacrifice unnecessary. The Old Testament sacrificial system was repetitive, requiring renewed sacrifices for new sins and for yearly cycles. This is another aspect that the author of Hebrews wants us to catch: Jesus's once-for-all sacrifice is a fulfillment that renders the previous system complete and no longer necessary.

Various models exist, attempting to draw together various aspects of what happens on the cross. Sometimes theologians will put these systems against one another and argue for only one. However, each system points to something true about the atonement, and finding ways to combine these systems is helpful. In other words, rather than seeking one system to encapsulate what the atonement is, we can recognize that various pictures help us see different vital, irreplaceable aspects of what is happening on the cross.

One of the most helpful recent attempts at this sort of approach is in the work of Joshua McNall's *Mosaic of Atonement*.[1] Because the New Testament itself contains several pictures of the atonement, McNall encourages us not to select one, but to better understand how these various pictures relate to make one larger picture. Just as multi-colored tiles are put together to create a larger picture, these pictures of the work of Christ, when properly related, give us a fuller picture of what the atonement is. We will work through McNall's treatment here.

First, the feet of the image are recapitulation theories of the atonement. Recapitulation theories rightly situate Jesus's life and his death on the cross within the larger story of God's work with the people of Israel. In other words, Jesus did not come out of nowhere to die on a cross to save sinners. Instead, he came out of a history of God's revelation and working with his people, and God

---

[1] Joshua McNall, *The Mosaic of Atonement: An Integrated Approach to Christ's Work* (Grand Rapids: Zondervan Academic, 2019).

has done things and worked in ways that were meant to point forward to Jesus. Jesus, then—in his life, death, and resurrection—picked up and recapitulates these aspects of the story, further developing their meaning and providing salvation. Recapitulation theories pick up on places in the Gospels where Jesus is presented as the New Adam, New Moses, and New Israel. In these instances, we see Jesus's faithful obedience in places where these earlier figures fell short or were incomplete. Paul picks up this idea of Jesus as the New Adam in Romans 5. We see Jesus as a New Moses in Matthew when he goes up on a mountain, sits down, and gives a law that can be divided into five. Jesus is the New Israel when he goes through the water (baptism) and then is tempted in the wilderness but does not give in and sin (Matt 4:1–11). In these acts of recapitulation, Jesus established solidarity with Israel and with all humanity. His ultimate act of recapitulation, then, happened on the cross, where he identified with humanity in his acceptance of punishment for sin.

McNall presents the penal substitution theory next as what he calls the "heart" of the atonement. At the most basic level, this theory is that on the cross Jesus accepted and paid the penalty for sin on behalf of sinful people (hence, "penal"). Jesus did not simply represent us in a loose way as with recapitulation; he also served as our formal substitute. The penalty is the one we deserve for punishment for breaking God's law, a penalty we bear as individual members of the sinful human race, as well as for our individual sins. The penalty Jesus bore was both for the original sin that infected the human race and for our individual sins that we commit as sinners. (Here is another place that we see the connections in theology—our understanding of the corporate and individual elements of sin informs the way we understand the penalty that Jesus pays on the cross for sin.) The penalty that Jesus pays is tied to the promises that God made in the Old Testament related to the consequences for breaking the covenant, for sin. God promised curses and demanded sacrifice. In sending Jesus to the cross, God did not change his mind, or take back what he had said about sin or its seriousness. Rather, he took on himself the penalty. Jesus took on this penalty willingly, submitting to the will of the Father, even as he knew of the pain and suffering he would face because he was fully human (hence his prayer in the garden of Gethsemane in Matt 26:36–56).

Here we are set up to see one of the helpful aspects of McNall's "mosaic": penal substitution itself works with the logic of recapitulation. After all, sacrifice is not new in the New Testament; rather, Jesus's death for sins is built on and finds its meaning as an extension and fulfillment of the Day of Atonement specifically and the sacrificial system more broadly in the Old Testament. Penal substitution fits with the Bible's picture of God as a covenant-keeping God, a God who keeps his promises even when it costs him. When we think we want God to just "take back" the whole "punishment for sins" idea and just forgive without any penalty, we fail to realize that this would compromise justice, it would change the character of our unchanging God, and none of that is good news in the long run.

At the same time, this part of the mosaic creates confusion in our culture. Some would call this divine child abuse; it is a father abusing a son. But this violates the way Christians understand the very nature of God and the doctrine of the Trinity. This critique divides the Godhead and separates the persons. This "divine child abuse" critique—though rightly sensitive to issues of violence in our culture—oversimplifies and puts the worst reading on Jesus's own words. In a way, this critique of the atonement shows us more about our culture than it does anything about the atonement. It shows that in our violent and broken culture, we have a hard time conceiving of self-sacrifice, or taking another's penalty, or there even being penalties at all because of how we have seen such ideas abused by fallen humans. Jesus's death on the cross should not be seen as an example encouraging abuse; rather, it demonstrates the seriousness of sin and the penalty that is due to all who break God's law, including those who violently disrespect the image of God in their fellow human beings.

Next is the head: Christus Victor theories. Atonement theories in this category emphasizes Jesus's victory on the cross. He is triumphant over Satan and evil powers. He defeats death in his death and resurrection. He accomplishes our salvation, and points forward to the ultimate victory of reuniting sinners with their Creator. Here again we see the necessity of connecting the various pictures of the atonement together to understand what is going on. Why is Jesus's death victorious? His victory is centered on reuniting sinners with God, and that victory requires the logic of recapitulation to work. Additionally, the only reason Jesus can provide this victory is by taking on sin and its penalty, as emphasized in the penal substitution theory. In other words, Jesus's victory does not happen in isolation from other theories of the atonement. And it does not happen in isolation from other doctrinal issues—it is a victory *over* sin; it is a victory *for* salvation; it is a sacrifice *for* the church.

The hands are the fourth and final piece of the mosaic. This piece covers moral influence theories of the atonement. According to these explanations of the cross, we understand the work of Christ on the cross when we understand its moral impact. This impact is explained in a few different ways. For some, the cross is a display of the radical love of God. This display motivates, inspires, and fuels moral living by believers. In other words, this theory on its own says that the cross did not need to pay any penalty, but it inspires on the basis of God's love for us. Another version that fits in this category would be moral government theories, which emphasize God is demonstrating that sin is something he takes very seriously when Jesus dies on the cross. The power of the atonement in both of these examples lies in its ability to communicate a truth that is meant to shape and guide human morality—love or the seriousness of sin.

On their own, moral influence theories leave out key aspects of what the Bible says about the cross. And, in some ways, they leave out key aspects that the theories themselves depend upon! It is true that God's great love for us is displayed on the cross, as Paul himself said (Rom 5:6–11), as did John (1 John 4:10). But that love is only properly seen when we understand Christ's role as the head of what Paul calls the "New Adam" (Romans 5) and when we understand that the penalty had to be paid. Jesus taking on our penalty shows love. Jesus enduring violence for the sake of extravagant illustration communicates something different. In addition, the idea of God's moral government of the universe is tied in with justice for sin, which requires connection to other theories of the atonement. In short, these moral theories are significant right where McNall places them: the hands of a bigger picture. The atonement should press us into a moral response to God but is a response that is not only rooted in the cross of Christ, it is made possible by the ongoing work of the Holy Spirit. God the Father sweeps people up into his work, through the work of Christ, and through the work of the Holy Spirit. The Spirit makes us into the body of Christ, the body of Jesus, as we'll consider when we get to Ecclesiology. In other words, through the cross, through the power of the Holy Spirit, through salvation, God makes us look like Jesus.

God also brings us into the work of Jesus. This is where ethics is properly located. This is where ecclesiology, the doctrine of the church, comes into play, and the last things, eschatology. The Spirit makes us into the body of Jesus. There is a moral influence on the cross. The cross does reform us, quite literally. It reforms us into the image of the Son. That transformation absolutely has a moral influence on us. We can say that the victory won on the cross by Jesus's vicarious representation and penalty bearing is worked out in our bodies, making them into a "Body" to bear witness to the world of the breaking in of the kingdom of God.

Do you see how this mosaic works? Feet, heart, head, hands. It provides a helpful way to conceptualize how different biblical pictures of Jesus's work on the cross fit together to give us a better sense of the whole. We need the recapitulation piece, because we need that to explain why a first-century Jewish carpenter turned rabbi has anything to do with us and our relationships with God. He is the New Adam. As Paul reminds us in Romans 5, the One in whom we have hope, the hope of salvation, is getting moved from being in Adam to Christ. We need that recapitulation piece to explain, "Why does the crucifixion have anything to do with me?"

Second, we need this idea of substitution for a penalty. If we are going to consistently read Jesus as someone who has something to do with God's story in Scripture, and if we're going to have the Old Testament be anything besides God "twiddling his thumbs," waiting to send his Son, we have to understand this notion of penalty, this notion of covenant, this gracious and merciful notion of Jesus choosing to stand in and bear our sin, and the Father punishing sin, not the Son.

Third, we must remember the victory that Christ has won. We cannot think of Jesus as only a victim, even though he is. He bears sin and evil, but he is also victorious through that. He sweeps us up into that victory. He brings us with him. When we get to the doctrine of salvation, we will deal with how Paul, over and over, speaks of believers as "in Christ."

Finally, we need this picture of the hands, the piece that reminds us that God does not only save us to leave us alone, but God saves us to reform us, to unite us to Christ, and to each other.

CONCLUSION

As noted earlier, to understand the work of Christ, we must understand the person of Christ. Jesus's work as prophet, priest, and king can only hold together in light of his one person, fully human and fully divine. We must also connect the work of Christ to its purpose. The death of Christ is nothing less than the death of the God-Man, *for us and for our salvation*. And that work of salvation begins with the work of the Holy Spirit. We will turn to these two topics next: first, the Holy Spirit, and then the Spirit's work of salvation in us.

═══════════

The Challenge of the Atonement in Law Practice
GREGORY JORDAN

For the Christian in any calling, whether it is social, political, educational, business, or even the ministry, there is an existential conflict between living the kingdom principles as taught in the New Testament and following the basic value assumptions set by the work. Especially in law practice, the atonement should bring liberty in an ethical sense to the practitioner, but it more frequently creates a challenge and, possibly, a crisis of faith.

As Dallas Willard has taught, chief among the meanings of atonement in the gospel is the eternal kind of life exemplified by Jesus, a life of the intimate involvement of God as revealed in the entire biblical tradition.[2] To cite only one of many passages illuminating such a life we have:

> Beloved, let us love one another, for love is from God, and whoever loves has been born of God and knows God. Anyone who does not love does not know God, because God is love. In this the love of God was made manifest among us, that God sent his only Son into the world, so that we might live through him. In this is love, not that we have loved God but that he loved us and sent his Son to be the propitiation for our sins. Beloved, if God so loved us, we also ought to love one another. No one has ever seen God; if we love one another, God abides in us, and his love is perfected in us.
>
> By this we know that we abide in him and he in us, because he has given us of his Spirit. And we have seen and testify that the Father has sent his Son to be the Savior of the world. Whoever confesses that Jesus is the Son of God, God

---

[2] Dallas Willard, *The Divine Conspiracy: Rediscovering Our Hidden Life in God* (Harper Collins: New York, 1997), 42–50.

abides in him, and he in God. So we have come to know and to believe the love that God has for us. God is love, and whoever abides in love abides in God, and God abides in him. By this is love perfected with us, so that we may have confidence for the day of judgment, because as he is so also are we in this world. There is no fear in love, but perfect love casts out fear. For fear has to do with punishment, and whoever fears has not been perfected in love. We love because he first loved us. (1 John 4:7–19 ESV)

Colossians 3:12–15 is also particularly relevant. These passages reveal to us that Christ came to die and purchase us for eternal life, but they also reveal what he prophesies and teaches, and how he intends to rule us as members of the kingdom family. If we do not exhibit love for others, or humility, self-sacrifice, kindness, generosity, or forgiveness, we do not exemplify the atonement. If we are not sensitive to the needs of others, both physically and spiritually, we do not exemplify the atonement. The fruit of the Spirit are well-known to us from Scripture (Gal 5:22–23). Christ taught all these things not as compartmentalized Christian virtues to be set aside in the crush of the practice of law but as the central guiding force of life of the child of the kingdom. Clearly then, the earthly assumptions behind every human endeavor are weighed in the balance against these eternal truths and found wanting.

The following prayer of Jesus reveals much about the expected tension between the two worldviews:

And I am no longer in the world, but they are in the world, and I am coming to you. Holy Father, keep them in your name, which you have given me, that they may be one, even as we are one. While I was with them, I kept them in your name, which you have given me. I have guarded them, and not one of them has been lost except the son of destruction, that the Scripture might be fulfilled. But now I am coming to you, and these things I speak in the world, that they may have my joy fulfilled in themselves. I have given them your word, and the world has hated them because they are not of the world, just as I am not of the world. I do not ask that you

take them out of the world, but that you keep them from the
evil one. They are not of the world, just as I am not of the
world. Sanctify them in the truth; your word is truth. As you
sent me into the world, so I have sent them into the world.
And for their sake I consecrate myself, that they also may be
sanctified in truth. (John 17:11–19 ESV)

As a practicing lawyer in business-related litigation, and as a teacher of
both law and ethics, I am continuously challenged by the contrast between
these kingdom goals of the Christian and the goals of justice in law. Justice
in the criminal law context involves punishment and restitution by the con-
victed to restore the fabric of humans living in society. Justice in the civil law
context between private parties involves both judicially coerced changes
in human behavior and awarded compensation to essentially restore the
balance in human (corporate) liberty. Of course, in the private law context,
agreements involving business and family relationships and endeavors, etc.,
do not have to be in open conflict, yet such agreements and negotiations are
essentially self-centered. They are protective. Therefore, the parties in the
conflicts become adversarial. They are focused on themselves only. They are
either trying to change the other party's behavior by forcing them judicially
to do or stop doing something, or they are trying to obtain money or property from them as compensation for some wrong done to them. The other
party of course is denying any responsibility, etc. Where is love? Where is
generosity? Where is forgiveness and considering others first?

It is the duty of the lawyers, the judges, and the legislators to represent
their clients and constituents in good faith, aggressively, and without conflict
of interest in achieving these goals. We become experts in our subject matter, and hone our craft, and strategize for the parties within the complexities
of the legal framework to guide our clients through the maze. We scheme
and plan and seek to force the other side into a corner that achieves our
client's self-interested goal. Such legal goals are manifestly contrary to the
passages in 1 John and Colossians cited above. Paul even demands that we
not sue each other in court. Hmmm . . . well, I would have to go find honest
work, as they say.

Yet, I have been comforted from time to time by realizing two truths.
One is that we live in a fallen world. A world that is ruled by evil temporarily.

We continue to try to achieve order in the chaos of human failure through the political and legal structures we create. And Jesus left us here to manage order and to bring the light of his eternal truth to such a world in anticipation of the eternal kingdom of God. The high priestly prayer above as captured by John is clear. So, I have in many ways found peace in realizing that until the Second Coming we humans will remain essentially self-centered and afraid. The invisible church inhabited by the redeemed is called within each profession to show love in the ways Christ showed love.

There is no handy template in each case by which the lawyers and the parties should reestablish order between them consistent with the doctrine of the atonement. We have been given minds and training to use to judge each situation in light of these existential contests. More importantly, we have been given the Holy Spirit as a voice in our hearts. The best we can do through Christ is the best we can do. As long as we accept our weaknesses and rely on him, we will come as close as possible to the kingdom goals in the world where Christ left us. Romans 8 comforts us here.

I experienced many professions in my representation of private parties over thirty years of law practice. My observation is that every Christian professional, including lawyers, is at risk of failing to see the conflict between the tenets of our faith and the underlying goals of the profession. And it goes without saying that trying to beat the competition and make as much money as possible falls into this category. My goal as a Christian teacher is to open students' eyes to the conflict between their Christian duty and the world's standards and, at the same time, to give them tools for managing the worldly goals of business and law. Jesus saw this coming in John 17.

Is this a failure to see the truth and an excuse to keep on living the life of a lawyer? I am not sure. But as long as I know I need his help, I can hopefully reveal him even to my adversaries.

Related Scripture

Isaiah 52:13–53:12
Matthew 27:32–54
Luke 24:1–12
John 3:14–21
Acts 1:6–11

Romans 5:1–21
Colossians 2:9–15
1 Timothy 2:3–6
Hebrews 9:11–28

<hr>

FURTHER READING

Letham, Robert. *The Work of Christ*. Downers Grove, IL: IVP, 1993.

Macleod, Donald. *Christ Crucified: Understanding the Atonement*. Downers Grove, IL: IVP Academic, 2014.

McNall, Joshua. *The Mosaic of Atonement: An Integrated Approach to Christ's Work*. Grand Rapids: Zondervan, 2019.

Stott, John R. W. *The Cross of Christ: 20th Anniversary Edition*. Downers Grove, IL: IVP, 2006.

Wright, N. T., Simon Gathercole, and Robert Stewart. *What Did the Cross Accomplish?: A Conversation about the Atonement*. Louisville: Westminster John Knox, 2021.

8

Holy Spirit

The doctrine of the Holy Spirit has enjoyed something of a revival of interest in the last 100 years—a revival that makes it both easier and harder to discuss, especially in a book aimed at broad evangelical thought. Scholars trace an academic recovery of this doctrine through Schleiermacher and Barth, and the advent and growth of various Pentecostal and charismatic denominations have brought the topic into the center of practical ministry concerns too. This phenomenon not only infused new denominations with growth; it also challenged existing churches and denominations to consider more carefully how Christians should look for, long for, and expect the Holy Spirit to work.

Two temptations loom.[1] First, we may be tempted to marginalize the doctrine of the Holy Spirit. In the West, we live in an age when belief in anything called a "spirit" is suspect. Christians can feel a bit strange focusing on this doctrine and therefore set it off to the side a bit. Additionally, the fact that many Christians disagree about how the Holy Spirit works today can lead to calls to marginalize this doctrine. "Let's focus on our areas of agreement" has many strengths, but it also leads to marginalizing many important doctrines when we not only avoid talking about our disagreements, but we stop discussing the doctrine altogether. Second, we may be tempted to depersonalize the Holy Spirit. This happens when we make our talk of the Holy Spirit vague, something akin to "spirituality," as though the Spirit is some force or impersonal source of power in churches. The Holy Spirit is not some spiritual utility that we plug into to charge our spiritual batteries. As Christians, we must avoid both of these temptations by giving appropriate attention to the Third Person of the Trinity. And as I will argue in this chapter, the very nature of the

---

[1] Millard Erickson discusses some of these difficulties. See *Introducing Christian Doctrine*, 3rd ed., 297.

work that the Holy Spirit does puts us in a place where we must pay attention to these temptations. We cannot seek solutions that betray the very work the Spirit does. But more on that later.

PERSON

To better understand the Holy Spirit, we will follow the same split between "person" and "work" that we did when we explored Christology. The Holy Spirit is divine. The Spirit is God to the same degree that the Father is God, and the Son is God. God reveals this truth to us in various ways in Scripture. For instance, in Acts 5, two believers named Ananias and Sapphira (a husband and wife) sell a piece of property and claim to give all the money to the church. When their lie is found out, Peter first says that Ananias had lied to the Holy Spirit, and a few verses later says that he had lied to God. Peter is not expanding the list here: well, first you lied to the Holy Spirit, but it gets worse! Then you lied to God! No, the clear meaning of the text is that the Holy Spirit is God. In lying to the Holy Spirit, they lied to God. Additionally, Paul provides us interesting insight into the person of the Holy Spirit in 1 Cor 2:10–11. There, he talks of the Holy Spirit searching everything, even the depths of God. According to Paul, no one can comprehend the thoughts of God except God. Therefore, the flow of this argument builds upon and emphasizes the full divinity of the Holy Spirit. We could go on with other examples, such as the book of Hebrews, which speaks of the Holy Spirit as eternal (Heb 9:14), and the book of Luke, which talks of the Holy Spirit as the power of God (Luke 1:35), an idea in the divine world that would have clearly communicated the Spirit's divine nature. He is not part God, or junior God. He is God.

We also must realize that the Holy Spirit is a person, not a force. Christians often slip and use the pronoun "it" for the Holy Spirit. But a person is not an "it," and by using "it" we are lying about the Holy Spirit! The Holy Spirit is a person. The Spirit is not a force. The Spirit is given personal things to do; Jesus talks about the Spirit as a comforter (John 14:26). That is something that a person does, not a force. The Spirit has personal characteristics such as intelligence, will, and emotion. The Spirit teaches in John 14, has a will in 1 Corinthians 12, and can be grieved in Ephesians 4. Further, in the New Testament we see writers going out of their way to emphasize the Spirit's personhood, even using unconventional grammar to do so. In Greek, pronouns match the gender of the noun they are referring to (and every noun has a grammatical gender). Proper grammar uses a feminine pronoun to refer to a feminine noun, or a masculine pronoun, or a neuter pronoun, as dictated by particular words. The word for "spirit" in Greek is a neutral word, but the New Testament always uses the masculine pronoun when referring to the Holy Spirit. In other words, we could say that the New Testament writers wanted to teach us not to call the Holy Spirit an "it," even if grammatical rules press in that direction. The Holy Spirit is a person. He is God. He gets the same honor as the other persons, and he is one with the Father and the Son. Also, since the Spirit dwells within believers (1 Cor 3:16), we are constantly reminded that God is not far off; rather, he has drawn quite near.

WORK

As we talk about the work of the Holy Spirit, we need to remind ourselves of what we have already learned about the Trinity. God is one God, eternally existing in three persons: Father, Son, and Spirit. Early church theologians emphasized the unity of the godhead with the idea that the working of God is not completely divided between persons. In other words, when we talk about one person of the Trinity working, we should not think about that work happening in the total absence of the other two persons. The unity of the Trinity makes that impossible. When the Father works, God works. When the Son works, God works. When the Spirit works, God works. At the same time, it is appropriate to talk about the persons working in that way. We just need to be cautious not to introduce too much division between the persons by imagining them working in isolation from the other two persons. When we talk about the working of the Holy Spirit, then, we are acknowledging the role that the Holy Spirit as a person plays in the triune God's ways of redemption. This truth also reminds us that when the Father works, and the Son works, the Holy Spirit is not silent and inactive but also caught up in that same work of the triune God.

Two general ideas encompass the Holy Spirit's ways of working.[2] First, the Holy Spirit perfects. On one hand, this means that the Holy Spirit works to take broken people and fix them. We see this work of the Holy Spirit in the work of

---

[2] I owe this "ways of working" approach to Michael Horton. See his *Rediscovering the Holy Spirit: God's Perfecting Presence in Creation, Redemption, and Everyday Life* (Grand Rapids: Zondervan Academic, 2017).

salvation, for instance, which we will talk about in more detail in the next chapter. But that is not the primary way of perfecting. The Holy Spirit takes something that is incomplete and brings it to completion, to perfection in the sense of reaching a goal rather than simply overcoming a deficiency. In other words, the Holy Spirit works in all things in God's creation to bring them to their designed and desired perfection, complete and whole and rightly connected to God and all things. This overall work of perfecting is where we see the Spirit's work of judgment and justification too. In John 16 the Spirit is described as an advocate or attorney, who convicts the world of sin. In his judgment, the Spirit convicts of sin so that people turn from sin to Christ and begin to bear fruit. In his judgment, the Holy Spirit both judges and brings fruit. He convicts of sin, and then he causes us to bear fruit. This is all in his work of perfecting. The Spirit cleanses us of sin; the Spirit preserves us. These are acts of perfecting.

Along with the perfecting work of the Holy Spirit, Scripture speaks of the indwelling work of the Holy Spirit. Obviously, these are related because the Spirit indwells believers and thereby perfects them. At the same time, this way of working is important to highlight because of its significance for understanding salvation and the Christian life. The Holy Spirit indwells God's people. We see this in the Old Testament when the Holy Spirit indwelled certain people for certain purposes for certain periods of time (1 Sam 16:14, for example, speaks of the Holy Spirit leaving Saul). The prophets pointed forward to a time when all of God's people would experience hearts of flesh and the indwelling of God's Spirit.

One way that we see this indwelling work is in the ability to remember and understand God's Word. Jesus promised that he would send the Spirit, who would help the disciples remember what Jesus had taught (John 14:26). Additionally, the Holy Spirit opens eyes, ears, and hearts to see, hear, and love God's Word. These actions are not something people achieve on our own, but because of the indwelling work of the Holy Spirit. This work extends beyond the individual believers to the work, growth, and ministry of the church, which is composed of believers.

We also see that the Spirit works to illuminate the church so that believers can understand and embrace God's Word. He accomplishes this without coercion. This idea points us back to the mysterious way in which God can fully be in control, while created things can truly be free, which we discussed when considering concursus. Created things operate under God's sovereignty while being truly free to act in accord with the type of creatures that they are. Part of the Spirit's work is guiding us, illuminating our eyes, and shaping our hearts so that we can embrace God's will without coercion. The Holy Spirit does not force us to do what we do not want to do, but rather he gives us life and draws us to God through Christ's work. We have true freedom in that.

Now that we have looked at the general ways the Spirit works in perfecting and indwelling, we'll turn to more specific actions we see the Holy Spirit doing in Scripture. First, we see the Holy Spirit involved in creation. As one theologian puts it, he carries with him the plans of the Father and the materials purchased by the Son as he builds the sanctuary, according to all that he has received.[3]

The Spirit's way of working in creation extends beyond the creation account in the beginning of Genesis. Let us explore two examples of this. First, the Holy Spirit was at work in the construction—or creating—of the tabernacle in the Old Testament. God gave Moses precise instructions for how the tabernacle was to be built, and those instructions required a high degree of skill and ability. Creating what God commanded was not within the realm of possibility for Moses and the Israelites. The text tells us that God appoints and equips a man named Bezalel to serve as the chief artisan (see Exodus 31 and 36–39). Bezalel, then, uses the gifts that God gives him to create the tabernacle. While this might initially seem like a minor story in the Old Testament about early worship practices, it falls into this pattern of the way of the Holy Spirit's working: the Holy Spirit is at work in creation. The Holy Spirit works to create the tabernacle, where God visibly dwelt among his people as they wandered in the wilderness.

A second example connects to both creation and this first example, and it also sets us up to better understand the Holy Spirit's way of working today. As we will discuss in more detail when we explore the doctrine of salvation, the Holy Spirit is at work creating a people of God. The Spirit works to convict people of sin and equips them to turn from that sin to saving faith in Jesus Christ. When we connect this way of working to the other ways that the New Testament talks about the new covenant people of God, remarkable connections to Bezalel emerge. When the Holy Spirit works in salvation, he is working to build the church, which is described as the *body* of Christ and the *temple* of

---

[3] Horton, 47.

the Holy Spirit. Do you catch the connection? Just as the Holy Spirit worked in the creation of the tabernacle symbolizing God's presence among his Old Covenant people, the Holy Spirit also works in the construction of the church, which as a body of people—not a building—is called the "body of Christ" and is in a very real sense where we see the presence of God in the modern world. In both cases, the Spirit works to create something that demonstrates the fact that God has drawn near, that God redeems, that God reconciles.

Another helpful way to distinguish the various ways that the Holy Spirit works in the church today is to distinguish between the Spirit's extraordinary work and his ordinary work. Oftentimes, we think about his extraordinary work first and primarily, for various reasons. By extraordinary work I mean what many refer to as miraculous gifts or sign gifts—things like speaking in tongues, healing, interpreting tongues, and prophecy. The New Testament clearly marks such things as the work of the Holy Spirit, so we should rightly note that. We'll discuss these gifts in more detail below, since there are various ways to understand these extraordinary gifts today. But we easily associate them with the work of the Spirit, because it seems so obvious—what other explanation might there be? (Granted, some scholars study these phenomena from a naturalistic perspective and argue that they can be fully explained without reference to God or a spiritual world at all. My argument here is primarily concerned with Christians: most Christians see these sorts of gifts and think of the Holy Spirit, and when they think of the Holy Spirit they think of these gifts.) When we think of the Holy Spirit we think of this extraordinary work because of the testimony of Scripture and because of the continued testimony of such events in our world today.

While we shouldn't shy away from the Holy Spirit's extraordinary work, we also shouldn't downgrade the Spirit's ordinary work. By ordinary work, I mean the day-in-and-day-out work in the spiritual lives of believers, work that Scripture reveals to us but that we often take for granted. The Holy Spirit's work in salvation—in turning rebels against God into children of God—is a truly remarkable work, and one that we rely on the Holy Spirit for. But we do not usually see it as exciting as the extraordinary work. Additionally, the Holy Spirit's work in the lives of believers—slowly sanctifying them and transforming them to look like Christ as a result of their faith in Christ—often falls out of our imaginations when we think of the Holy Spirit. We often feel these changes as our own achievements, but they are not. The Holy Spirit works these aspects of growth in the life of the believer, even as the believer works hard to grow as well. This is the dynamic that Paul gets at when he commands the Philippian church to "work out" their salvation "with fear and trembling," reminding them that in fact it is "God who works in you" (Phil 2:12–13). When the Spirit brings fruit in our lives, it does not always seem as extraordinary as some of the miraculous gifts do. But, according to Scripture, it is in fact just as extraordinary, just as reliant upon the work of God, the work of the Holy Spirit. Any division we insert between the miraculous gifts, which strike us as extraordinary, and the everyday gifts of fruit, which can strike us as mundane, is our own doing, and something that we must be careful about. Seeing someone turn from darkness to light, to slowly grow in the fruit of the Spirit, is no less a work of God than miraculous healing.

MAPPING CONTROVERSY

Let's dive into the miraculous gifts a bit more deeply. Christian approaches to these miraculous gifts have spawned new denominations over the last 100 years as well as created different strains within existing denominations. On one hand, a growing number of Christians—often labeled Pentecostal or charismatic—have come to see these miraculous gifts as necessary signs of salvation and blessing. For these believers, the pattern of a second "baptism of the Holy Spirit," observed among some believers in the book of Acts, is a normal pattern that must mark all true believers today. Furthermore, healings and speaking in tongues should be expected as regular marks of the Spirit's work in the church as well.

For other Christians, these miraculous gifts played a unique role during the time when the gospel first began to spread, and they do not characterize regular Christian life today. At the most basic level, "cessationists" argue that the miraculous gifts have ceased, because they served a special purpose for the early church. Their purpose was to verify the power and truth of the gospel in its earliest days as it began to spread. As the thinking goes, once Christianity emerged from its earliest days, it no longer required these sign gifts to mark its power and authority. Since they were no longer needed and they do not serve that purpose anymore, they should not be part of the regular Christian walk.

As is often the case, some Christians seek a middle ground. According to this way of thinking, the miraculous gifts do indeed serve a clear purpose in

Scripture, but that purpose is still needed today. While not every believer will experience these miraculous gifts, we should not be surprised when they occur, especially in societies where the gospel is first breaking in. In that case, the gifts serve the same role as they did in the early church, but they do not become something that must always in every culture and church mark the spread of the gospel in the same way.

The above is a necessary simplification of a wide variety of actual denominations, local churches, and individual Christians. Yet it is useful as a map: showing the general territories and their borders, without classifying absolutely everything about each detail on the map. My goal here is not to convince you of a place to be on this map, but to help you locate yourself and then to evaluate whether your expectations of the Holy Spirit's way of working align with what Scripture reveals.

I think one question can help get to the key aspects of whether any particular perspective, or miraculous working, is the work of the Holy Spirit or not. That question is this: Who is the center of attention in this? According to Scripture, the Holy Spirit's job is to convict the world of sin, point them to Christ, and help believers know and follow the teachings of Christ. The Spirit's goal is not to draw attention to himself. The Spirit's goal is to be a comforter; the Spirit's goal and role is to point to the finished work of Christ. When we see these miraculous gifts, or when we see these things that are claiming to be the work of the Spirit we must ask if it lines up with what the Holy Spirit does— draw attention to Christ. This is true whether it is the extraordinary work or the ordinary work of the Holy Spirit, whether it is the Spirit's work of judgment, or perfecting, or whatever else we might find useful in describing what the Holy Spirit does.

CONCLUSION

This chapter serves as an excellent example of what theological study does. At its best, it does not leave us with all our questions answered. Hopefully, as we seek the face of God in Scripture and in the testimony of brothers and sisters in Christ— whether living or long dead—we find some of our questions answered. At the same time, we hope that we have other, perhaps better or more mature, questions kindled within us. It is those questions that drive us to worship—worship that finds itself in awe of God and also worship that manifests as a pursuit of deeper knowledge about who God has revealed himself to be.

The Holy Spirit and Psychology
SARAH J. BRACEY

The field of psychology encompasses several perspectives on human behavior. For many years, these orientations hinged their understanding of human psychology on how much emphasis they gave to the nature versus nurture debate. For example, the foundations of behaviorism were built on an understanding of nurture that human beings are a *tabula rasa* at birth upon which the world writes. Similarly, the foundations of humanism and sociocultural theories also stressed the impact that man's upbringing, experiences, and culture has upon his psychology.

Other orientations tended to focus on the nature side (psychodynamic, biological), which argue that humans are born with certain predispositions that will, consequently, impact their psychology. In more recent years, research has leaned more towards a both/and understanding of this debate. Yes, men and women are composed of their own genetics, hormones, and brain structures. However, they are also influenced by families and culture. Psychologists often refer to this approach as the *biopsychosocial* model of psychology. Humans are composed of their biology, their psychology, and their sociology. However, Christians may contest that this picture is not whole.

Eric Johnson asserts that we find a more complex understanding of human behavior in Scripture, compared to what modern psychology outlines.[4] Christian psychologists also take into consideration the possibility of spiritual, or supernatural, causes where God may be involved. Consequently, in seeking to understand human psychology, we study a more encompassing model that views humans as biopsychosocial *spiritual* beings. Thomas Oden, for example, wrote about Saint Augustine, who lived during the early fifth

---

[4] Eric L. Johnson, *God and Soul Care: The Therapeutic Resources of the Christian Faith* (Downers Grove, IL: IVP Academic, 2017), 105.

century, and proposed that Christians could receive counsel and comfort not only from Holy Scripture but also from the Holy Spirit.[5]

Defining "the doctrine of the Holy Spirit" is a wieldy task for which, unfortunately, time and space do not presently allow. Even within the evangelical tradition, various denominations may disagree on the nature or agency of the Spirit. However, most Christians tend to agree on certain elements as derived from biblical passages. For example, we see the arrival of the Holy Spirit in Acts 2 (Pentecost), which Jesus had previously foretold would occur (John 14:16). Christians receive the indwelling of the Spirit (1 Cor 12:7), along with particular gifts or services (vv. 8–10). Together, we make up the body of Christ (1 Cor 12:12–31) and, with these gifts, we grow and equip one another (Eph 4:15–16). Paul, in his letter to the Galatians, says that we are to "walk by the Spirit" to avoid fleshly desires (Gal 5:16) and, doing so, will produce the fruit of the Spirit (vv. 22–23).

Scripture references the Holy Spirit as the "Paraclete" (John 14:16, 26; 15:26; 16:7–11, 12–15), which translators have rendered as intercessor, advocate, comforter, and helper.[6] Abraham Kuyper speaks to the ministry of the Spirit, saying, "God's house, God's temple, God's dwelling place is no longer on Mount Zion, but in the heart of those who belong to Jesus."[7] After the fall, Johnson explains, God planned to restore humans to their original wholeness in Christ through the indwelling of the Holy Spirit.[8] Kuyper also comments on the importance of God's Spirit in man's redemption, explaining, "It is no longer a God far away, but a God close by—indeed, a God who dwells within our own heart."[9]

Within the field of psychology lie several subfields that focus on individual elements of the biopsychosocial model, but for the purposes of discussing the Holy Spirit, no subdiscipline is more suitable than that of counseling. "Advocate, comforter, helper" are terms that describe a mental health practitioner. If Christian counselors practice with the knowledge that their clients

[5] Thomas C. Oden, *Classical Pastoral Care: Pastoral Counsel*, Vol. 3: Classical Pastoral Care Series (Grand Rapids: Baker Academic, 1987), 103.

[6] "Paraclete," *Merriam-Webster*, https://www.merriam-webster.com/dictionary/Paraclete.

[7] Johnson, *God and Soul Care*, 465.

[8] Johnson, 107.

[9] Abraham Kuyper, *Pro Rege: Living under Christ's Kingship*, vol. 1, *The Exalted Nature of Christ's Kingship*, ed. John Kok with Nelson D. Kloosterman, trans. Albert Gootjes (Bellingham, WA: Lexham, 2016), 467.

are also spiritual beings, then he or she will recognize they are not the only agent of change within the therapeutic relationship. "All therapy involves at least two human persons," writes Johnson. "Christian therapy is distinguished by the explicit involvement of at least three persons—two human and one divine."[10] Thus God's Spirit is an agent of change who may speak to the client or through the counselor to the client.[11]

Some may argue against the notion of professional therapy, if indeed Christians have this indwelling "counselor." While the Holy Spirit should be a substantial influence on a Christian's healing process,[12] counselors can provide education and guidance that may help expedite the process. Learning how to reframe one's destructive thinking patterns, addressing feelings of false shame and guilt, and incorporating healthy boundaries are all examples of therapeutic processes that can take place alongside the Spirit's healing. Johnson points out that developing new neural networks and rewiring the brain takes time, which is why Christian counseling uses other means, too, that help facilitate these processes like prayer, Bible reading, meditation, music, fellowship, and church involvement.[13] Oftentimes, a person sees, perhaps for the first time, the "other-oriented love of the Spirit" through the therapeutic relationship of counselors, pastors, and spiritual directors.[14]

Christian counselors do not focus only on the spiritual sphere but also help to address the client's biology, psychology, and sociology. For example, a client may present with depression but, upon a referral to their general practitioner and some consequent bloodwork, come to find that the client is suffering from a thyroid issue. In this way, modern psychology and its biopsychosocial approach provide a helpful perspective for Christian counselors to understand their clients better. Ideally, secular therapists would be trained to engage the spiritual component of the clients they are serving, and Christian counselors would be educated to understand their client's biology, psychology, and sociology.

---

[10] Johnson, *God and Soul Care*, 116.
[11] Oden, *Classic Pastoral Care*, 99.
[12] Johnson, *God and Soul Care*, 111.
[13] Johnson, 124.
[14] Johnson, 125.

Related Scripture

Genesis 1:1–2
Matthew 3:13–17
John 14:15–17
Acts 1:1–8
Acts 2:1–21
Acts 10:44–48
Romans 8:1–27
1 Corinthians 2:6–16
1 Corinthians 6:15–20
Galatians 5:13–26
Ephesians 1:11–14
Titus 3:3–7

FURTHER READING

Allison, Gregg R., and Andreas J. Köstenberger, *The Holy Spirit*. Nashville: B&H Academic, 2020.

Castelo, Daniel. *Pneumatology: A Guide for the Perplexed*. New York: T&T Clark, 2015.

Ferguson, Sinclair. *The Holy Spirit*. Downers Grove, IL: IVP, 1997.

Packer, J. I. *Keep in Step with the Spirit*. Wheaton, IL: Crossway, 2021.

Sanders, Fred. *The Holy Spirit: An Introduction*. Wheaton, IL: Crossway, 2022.

Thiselton, Anthony. *A Shorter Guide to the Holy Spirit: Bible, Doctrine, Experience*. Grand Rapids: Eerdmans, 2016.

9

Salvation

S *alvation* is one of those church words that we can take for granted, assume we understand, and just breeze right on by. We can then easily start to misunderstand salvation. However, as we slow down and examine salvation as a term, we will find that even the word itself provides us a helpful reminder of how we need to think about salvation, and where we need to connect it.

While we cannot know everything about a word simply based on its etymology, etymologies can help us understand key aspects of how concepts develop and become what they are. That is the case with salvation. The root of the word "salvation" is the same root for one of the Spanish responses to a sneeze: "Salud." That word translates to something like "To your health!" or simply "Health." This idea is the same idea that lies behind the word "salvation." It relates to the Latin "Salus," the goddess of safety and well-being. It can mean safety, well-being, welfare, or health. We often jump right from "salvation" to "save," but in doing so we often miss these broader undertones, which tell us something about what saving even means. In short, salvation is certainly complicated, but it is rooted in this idea of health.

GUIDEPOSTS: HUMANITY AND THE FALL

Let us press a little deeper here. What do you need to know to help someone become healthy? Well, you need to know what health would look like for this person, and then you need to diagnose what it is about them that is getting in the way of health. What does "healthy" look like, and what illness or problem is causing the person to fall short of health? Once that diagnosis is made, you can help the person toward health, toward safety. You can "save" them from their illness.

We need nothing less when we talk about the doctrine of salvation. If we are going to talk about the spiritual health—indeed the holistic health—of human beings, we must know what health looks like. And we need some idea of the diagnosis of the problem. You may have noticed we have covered some of these ideas: we have explored what it means to be human, and we have developed an understanding of sin and the problems it introduces. Salvation can only be understood in light of those realities: what humans are created to be, and what the problem is.

The reason that I am circling around this is because I want us to understand that if we are going to talk about Christian salvation, if we are going to talk about Christian health, we need to know a couple things. First, we need to know what is wrong. But we also need to know what "right" is supposed to look like. In other words, we recognize it when someone is sick. We must determine what is wrong. But before we can even determine what is wrong, before we even say someone is actually sick, we have to know what health looks like.

The doctrine of salvation presupposes and builds upon other doctrines, the doctrine of humanity being one, the doctrine of sin being another. Even the doctrine of the incarnation is related here because we talked about how Jesus is fully God and fully human. When we come to the doctrine of salvation and ask the question of what it means to be saved, we should expect the answer we arrive at to be consistent with and connected to those other pieces. Salvation is not just a Get Out of Jail Free card. It is related to human nature. It is related to human flourishing, and it is related to real human problems. Those are the problems that it is addressed to solve.

SALVATION: UNION WITH CHRIST

The New Testament centers the doctrine of salvation around one simple but profound idea: union with Christ. Here is one of the clearest examples:

Earlier we referred to Romans 5 as a key text for understanding the way that Adam's sin impacted humanity. In that passage, Paul is building an argument. The part about Adam is a key part, but it is not his main point. Rather, the main point is that salvation is offered in union with Christ, just as sin is a result of being united with Adam. Paul draws up two categories of people: those who are "in Adam," and those who are "in Christ." The offer of salvation is to be united with Christ through faith in him.

Union with Christ produces results in the life of the believer. Scripture talks about these results in various ways. Theologian Millard Erickson notes the three main characteristics in a very helpful way. He explains that the union with Christ is a judicial union, a spiritual union, and a vital union. "Judicial union" refers to the way that Scripture talks about Christ taking on our judgment and our taking on his righteousness. We will spell this out below under the topic of justification. "Spiritual union" reminds us that this union is a union of spirits achieved by the work of the Holy Spirit, but it is done in a way that does not extinguish the individual person. We will discuss this more below under the topic of sanctification. Finally, "vital union" points to the life-giving nature of this union with Christ. The growth and change in a believer are a result of this union. This is a vital point but also deeper than that. It is vital in the sense that it is life-giving. Christ's life flows into ours, renewing our inner nature, as Paul wrote in Romans 12 and 2 Corinthians 4. This vital union with Christ imparts spiritual strength to us. We will also discuss this further under the topic of sanctification below.

This union has implications. As Paul says in Romans, those in Christ now face no condemnation from God. Paul does not say this because he knows everything you are going to do in life, but because you are united with Christ through faith. It also means that we now live with strength, even in crisis and testing. The popular related verse is Phil 4:13, which reminds us that we can do all things through Christ, who strengthens us. Often, Christians turn to this verse for encouragement in any challenge they face, but Paul particularly has in mind that God gives us strength to suffer with Christ. Our union not only means we will suffer with Christ, but also that we will one day reign with him (2 Timothy 2). As you can see, this image of "union with Christ" connects clearly to the process and results of salvation.

As I mentioned earlier, one way to explain the doctrine of salvation is to walk through the "order of salvation." Often, this process can yield nearly a dozen distinct steps because there are key aspects of salvation that need to be explained. However, this approach can produce confusion and division as Christians disagree on individual explanations and ordering. For our purposes, it is important to cover these various ideas and the ways they can relate, and we'll do this by following a big-picture "order of salvation," with three main categories: subjective aspects (how salvation "happens" from the perspective of the believer), objective aspects (what God says he has accomplished or done on our behalf), and ongoing aspects (how salvation is worked out throughout a person's life and into eternity).

SUBJECTIVE ASPECTS: TURNING TO CHRIST

In *Practicing Christian Doctrine*, theologian Beth Felker Jones divides the doctrine of salvation into beginnings, justification, sanctification, and final redemption.[1] It is that general phrase "beginnings" that we are dealing with here, such topics as election, calling, repentance, faith, and conversion. The first issue we need to realize is that Scripture teaches something very clear about the beginning of salvation, and it is this: salvation does not begin with us. Salvation cannot begin with us because of the problem of sin. As we explored earlier in the book, sin has broken and infected humanity. Paul uses the language of "slaves to sin" (Rom 6:20). Our freedom begins with God, not with our own doing.

At its least controversial point, the doctrine of election reminds us that salvation does not start with human work. "Election" is most often associated with Reformed theology, but it is a simple Bible word that any Christian who takes the Bible as an authority must believe in because it is found throughout Scripture. We see God choosing a people in the Old Testament to bless and make a blessing to the nations. Acts 13:48 (KJV) tells us that "as many as were ordained" obtained eternal life. Romans 8:28 talks about those who are predestined—though Christians disagree on the first part, which states that God predestined those whom he "foreknew." Ephesians 1:4–6 says that God chose believers before the foundation of the world. First Peter uses the language of a "chosen race." So, the question is not whether election is part of a Christian order of salvation, but what that election is based on. Enter the basic disagreement: election is based on the mysterious decision of God (Reformed), election is based on God looking ahead and electing those who will choose him (Arminian), or, for some, election simply means God chose Christ, "picking" anyone who would choose to place their faith in Christ.

The next aspect of the beginning of salvation, or the subjective aspects of salvation, is calling. We use "calling" in various ways in the church, often to refer to a sense of what God has called a person to do with his life. Working in

---

[1] Beth Felker Jones, *Practicing Christian Doctrine: An Introduction to Thinking and Living Theologically* (Grand Rapids: Baker, 2014).

a university setting, this is a common topic of discussion. Within the doctrine of salvation, calling refers to both the general call that God makes through the gospel presented to all people and more specifically to the individual work that God does in the heart of individuals when they hear that presentation of the gospel.

Christians understand a person's ability to respond to that call in different ways. Both perspectives often lack nuance in their most popular expressions. Reformed theology is often caricatured as a system of theology that has God dragging people who do not love him into relationship because he has chosen and called them. That is unfair. A Reformed perspective does emphasize that it is God who gives new spiritual life, new hearts, according to his will. Popular versions of Arminian theology also veer off as well. Many people forget that Arminians believe all are slaves to sin, too, and cannot accept God's call on their own. However, they argue that prevenient grace—a grace that "goes before"—changes each sinful heart at least to the point where the person is at a neutral place when they hear God's call of salvation. The person could choose to accept or reject God, but grace has already worked on their heart to even get them to the point of being able to choose. Christians do not believe that sinful people, on their own, can or will turn to God or work their way to God. But we understand the working of God's grace in different ways. My interest in this work is not to convince you in one direction or the other, but to provide a more accurate "lay of the land" and, hopefully, cultivate in you a desire to work deeper into these matters.

Next, the term "calling" refers both to the general explanation of the gospel that is to go out to all, and the specific work of God on the heart of the person who hears the gospel and responds in faith. We might call the first simply the "gospel call," meaning the proclamation of the gospel message to sinners. This message can take different forms in presentation, but it includes the general outline of God, his creation, the reality of sin (and our personal responsibility for it), Jesus's full divinity and humanity, his perfect life, his death for our sin, his resurrection, and his promised return. Jesus commanded his disciples to carry this message to the end of the world, and to call people to repent and believe this message so that they might be forgiven and reconciled to God in Christ.

Second, the Bible also speaks of a specific call, which refers to the way that God works in some hearts to receive the general call of the gospel. We see this reality in such places as John 6. As Matthew Barrett puts it, "The Jews listening to him do not believe in him, no matter how many miracles he performs. They are spiritually blind, and though they think they are free, they live in bondage. They take offense at Jesus and start grumbling (like their forefathers in the wilderness) when Jesus says he is the 'bread that came down from heaven' (6:41). Jesus responds, 'Do not grumble among yourselves. No one can come to me unless the Father who sent me draws him' (6:43)."[2] God draws the sinner through this specific calling. The picture is God drawing people to him, not forcing or coercing.

At this point, we are entering territory where Christians differ on how to relate different terms. We see this here with calling. How do you account for sinners' inability to turn to God? How do you describe when God's work truly begins in the human heart? Most Christians want to hold together mysteries that we have referenced previously: God is sovereign and in control, and people are free and responsible. God works and humans respond in ways that do not violate either of those truths. Yet we struggle to articulate that, especially when it comes to salvation and the relationship between calling, regeneration (new birth), and conversion.

Regeneration is such a central doctrine for evangelical faith that many times people describe evangelicals as "born-again Christians." Sometimes we downplay how radical this new birth really is. First, we should not downplay it if we remember how serious sin is, how broken we are, and how much we need God. Second, we should recognize that the Bible teaches that even those who seem the most holy on the outside still need new birth. We see this in John 3, when Jesus talks with Nicodemus, a Pharisee. As a Pharisee, Nicodemus knew a lot about God and lived an upright life. He seems like the type of person who might have just needed a small tweak to be right with God. Faith, sure, but nothing too radical. But remember what Jesus told Nicodemus: "You must be born again." And when Nicodemus reacted and said, "Wait. That's a little extreme. Am I supposed to go back inside my mother and be born a second time?" Jesus did not say, "Oh, Nicodemus, just kidding. It isn't that serious." No, instead Jesus corrected his misunderstanding in thinking about physical birth, but he emphasized that this spiritual rebirth is no less miraculous, no

---

[2] Matthew Barrett, "Effectual Calling," TGC, accessed October 17, 2022, https://www.the gospelcoalition.org/essay/effectual-calling/.

less absurd. Rebirth, regeneration—we should think something just as radical as being physically born again. God reveals this to us in the Old Testament prophets in a different way. There God describes the problem as people having hearts of stone and needing brand-new hearts of flesh (Ezek 36:26). Stone hearts do not turn into fleshy hearts. God removes the hearts of stone and gives hearts of flesh. Regeneration is a miraculous work of God based on his grace, not on our own works.

OBJECTIVE ASPECTS: JUSTIFICATION

Now that we have covered salvation from the perspective of what happens with reference to the human person being saved, we will turn to consider salvation from the perspective of what God has achieved or done objectively. You are likely familiar with the leading idea here: justification.

The term "justification" emerges from the legal context, emphasizing our standing before God. Because we understand the doctrine of sin, we can see why our standing before God is important. Due to Adam's sin and our own sin, we stand guilty before God and deserving of punishment. Justification, however, changes this status because we are given the righteousness of Jesus Christ. "God imputes righteousness" to us (Rom 4:6 NKJV), which means he gives it to us through (but not earned by) our faith in Christ. God reveals this idea in a few ways in the New Testament. For instance, in Gal 3:27 he speaks of our being "clothed with Christ." This picture helps us understand imputation. When God looks at those who are in Christ, those who have Christ's righteousness imputed to them, he sees Christ's righteousness, not their unrighteousness. Therefore, when God pronounces us "justified," it is not a fiction, but truth. The sins that were on your account were put on Jesus, and Jesus took the penalty of them. The righteousness of Jesus is put on yours. That is always true. If you have faith in Christ, you are always saved because of the righteousness of Christ. The temptation there can be, *Oh, early in salvation I'm saved because of what Jesus did, but down the road, after I've been sanctified, God will look at me on my own terms, and I will be saved.* That is not true. You are never saved because of your good works, even the good works that God has for you in the future as you grow in holiness and serve him. Those are never on your account for why you are safe, and that is good news. It is always justification; it is always imputation.

Scripture also speaks of this objective aspect of salvation through the concept of adoption. Adoption happens at the same time as conversion, regeneration, justification, and union with Christ. We can distinguish logically between these, but not chronologically. Adoption changes our status, and it changes our condition. God declares our status changed; we are in the family of God. Adoption is also a new condition: one of being favored by God. Through adoption, we are restored to the relationship with God that humans lost. Adoption introduces a type of relationship with God, unique when compared to what humans in general have with him. The unbeliever simply does not have and cannot experience what the believer experiences as an adopted child of God. It is this adoption that brings us justification and forgiveness of sin, that brings reconciliation and true liberty and freedom. We have the inheritance of what the firstborn son—Jesus, the only Son of God—has as a firstborn son—which, in the historical context, would mean the greatest inheritance.

That is what we have in the New Testament picture of salvation. Because if the salvation—the health that we are provided—is meant to tell us something, it helps us see that the problem is not simply sinning. It is the alienation from God that is a result of that sin. Salvation does not just stop us from living a lifestyle of sin. It reunites us to that family, it gives us that inheritance, that relationship with God, that union with Christ, which itself then is a life-giving union that sanctifies us.

PROGRESSIVE ASPECTS: SANCTIFICATION

While the objective aspects of salvation focus on changes that happen once— we are declared righteous, God adopts us—there are also ongoing effects of this salvation that are rightly considered part of the doctrine of salvation as well. For if salvation is about health, it is not only about overcoming the consequences of sin; it is also about shaping us to overcome sin and to do right. If we consider again the picture of union with Christ, we will remember that this union is a life-giving union. It shapes us—indeed, remakes us—in the image of the Son of God.

The progressive aspects of salvation start with the general concept of "sanctification," or being made holy, being made like Christ. Justification means that we are always considered righteous by God because of Christ, and sanctification means that the Holy Spirit is working to make us righteous like Christ.

Sanctification is continuous throughout life, and we cooperate with it. We see this in places like Phil 2:12–13, where Paul both commands us to work out our own salvation and reminds us that it is God who works in us. We must take both aspects of this seriously: sanctification is something we must work at, but while we're working at it, we must at the same time recognize that it is God working in us ultimately. It is not our own doing. We see God's role again in places like 1 Thess 5:23, where Paul wrote, "May the God of peace sanctify you completely." But we also see our role. We depend on God, so there is a passive element to it, but there is also an active element. We strive to obey God. Romans 6:13 (KJV) captures this passive piece: "Yield yourselves to God." Romans 8:13 refers to the more active part: "Put to death the deeds of the body." Similarly, Heb 12:14 (ESV) says to "strive for holiness." God is always active, and yet we are not merely passive.

Sanctification looks different in different people. Just as no two people are identical, having the same talents or the same struggles, so their progress in being made into the image of Christ will not be the same. For some, God brings quick growth in holiness. For others, it is slow. For most, it is faster at some points in life, slower in others, and sometimes may even seem to go backward. Even though with the doctrine of sanctification we remind ourselves that God does work to make us holy, we also need to consistently remind ourselves that it is a process that looks different for different believers.

Christians have different views on how much sanctification we should expect in this life. Some traditions believe in some form of "perfectionism." Given the difficulties with this term, it might be more helpful to think of it as "complete sanctification." According to this perspective, Christians should work toward and expect sanctification to make them completely like Christ in this life, which could lead to extended periods of time living perfectly, or without sin. Other traditions believe that this level of perfection will only come after death.

PROGRESSIVE ASPECTS: PERSEVERANCE

This topic leads us to another progressive aspect of salvation: perseverance. The doctrine of perseverance deals with the question of whether a Christian can lose salvation. Two sample texts highlight the tension in the New Testament. On the one hand, in John 10, Jesus talks about believers as sheep that the

Father has given to him, the Good Shepherd. Jesus makes clear that no one can take the sheep from him, emphasizing their eternal security in his hand (John 10:28–30). On the other hand, New Testament letters wrestle with how believers should respond to those who abandon the faith. In places like 1 John 2:19, the logic is that those who leave the faith were never really part of the faith. Yet Hebrews 6 speaks of those who taste Christ and then turn from him, going so far as to say it is impossible for these people to be restored again to the faith. Some interpret this passage to also be talking about those who were never truly saved. However these passages are put together, three things are clear. First, it is Christ that holds those who believe, not believers who sustain themselves. Second, any rejection of Christ is serious, but especially that rejection that comes after a period of (at least seeming) acceptance. Third, Christians should expect and work toward growth in holiness in their lives.

PROGRESSIVE ASPECTS: GLORIFICATION

The final piece of progressive salvation represents the end of this process: glorification. We see Paul using this term in Rom 8:30, where he provides assurance and comfort to the Roman Christians that God will bring salvation to completion. Those who are justified will be glorified, conformed to the image of the Son (Rom 8:29). Glorification is the bringing to completion what God promises in Phil 1:6.

These progressive aspects of salvation, then, emphasize the ongoing process of being made like Christ. Believers are being made holy by the work of God in them, even as they work hard along with what God is doing. Believers persevere, as promised by Christ, because of the power of his work, not our own. Finally, this process continues until we are made fully like Christ, when we are glorified in the last days.

CONCLUSION

Salvation is a beautifully complex topic in Christian theology. On one hand, the offer of salvation can be expressed very simply: "Repent and believe," as Jesus himself put it in Mark 1:15. On the other hand, the fullness of this topic depends on our understanding of so many topics in doctrine. We must understand who God is, who humans were created to be, the problem sin introduced, and the promise that the Son offers. We also must understand the work of the Holy Spirit, and something about the future that God has promised. Salvation centers on the health, the healing, that God promises and provides in the person and work of Jesus Christ. What a glorious doctrine!

———————

Salvation and Social Work
JILL WELLS

How does the doctrine of salvation challenge particular issues, practices, or assumptions in your field of study?

The field of social work involves many levels of practice and many different populations of clients. The profession is made up of a variety of people who may or may not profess to be Christians. Christian social workers do struggle with some challenges in addressing particular issues, practices, and assumptions. In looking at the issues, those that involve a moral dilemma that counters what Scripture teaches brings about such challenges. These issues can be abortion, same-sex relationships, co-habitation, or abuse.

The assumptions in the field of social work translate into six core values. These values involve: service, social justice, dignity and worth of the person, the importance of human relationships, integrity, and competence. Interestingly, these core values reflect Christian principles, presenting little challenge with these foundational values in the field.

The biggest challenge lies in the practice of social work. The profession of social work is governed by a code of ethics that directs how a social worker can practice. A social worker cannot in any way impose his or her own personal beliefs on a client. A social worker must validate and support a client's belief system whatever that involves. There must be a nonjudgmental approach with clients. For the Christian social worker, there is often an internal conflict when clients live a lifestyle that counters Christianity. However, those conflicts must be set aside. Every client is served regardless of his or her lifestyle choices or beliefs. An unconditional and caring approach is always extended to all clients.

How does your field of study provide a unique perspective or way of thinking that can help Christians better understand this doctrine or related topics?

Social work provides a unique perspective to help Christians understand the doctrine of salvation. As noted in this chapter, salvation is built upon the doctrine of humanity and sin. Human nature can be quite ugly. The social impact of sin is evident through such things as domestic violence, child abuse, alcohol, and drug addiction, as well as sexual assault and criminal actions. These behaviors all stem from sin. Sin creates an unhealthy person and society. The good news is, as also noted in this chapter, the root word in salvation, "Salus," means well-being and health. The goal in the practice of social work is to restore a person's well-being. Often this can involve counseling to address a behavior change or resources to meet a need. For example, if a person is struggling with addiction or a new diagnosis of diabetes, it is a daily battle to adopt new behaviors or transform bad behaviors into more productive ones. So, to assist someone to be "healthy" requires us to educate them on what healthy looks like. The ultimate outcome is to mirror this image of salvation by helping clients to restore their well-being and health.

The theoretical view utilized in social work is known as the "person in environment." This model sees a person as interconnected with systems. You cannot separate a person from their environment. They are impacted by their family, neighborhood, friends, and community. So, when a person makes a change to be healthy, this flows into all these relationships. Relationships are one key area of intervention for social work. If a parent or spouse is being abusive, we help teach them what healthy behaviors look like. This too happens when a person accepts salvation. Their life is changed and thus relationships change. The process of salvation which involves a continual "renewing of the mind" is very similar to the process of change in clients. When people are "reformed" or "recovered," this mirrors our image of salvation. The old ways of living have now been changed to adopt a healthier way to manage life in general.

In social work, we use a framework known as the "strengths perspective." Clients have external and internal resources for change. Many clients utilize their spiritual beliefs as their strength for change. For clients who accept salvation and the hope it brings, this is a significant source of strength for managing a social issue. Their faith allows them to have resilience through grief, trauma, or ongoing struggles with finances or relationships. If a behavior change is needed, this involves self-motivation whether that person is a Christian or not. It may require negative reinforcement such as probation, rehabilitation, or removal of children. It can also be positive interventions such as obtaining a job, housing, or resources to manage an illness. How clients respond to their situation and utilize their strengths impacts their change.

The historical foundation for social work practice has its roots in Christianity. Many of the early programs in the 1800s that served the poor and immigrants were faith-based. The church met many needs before any government programs were created. The field of social work truly represents what many Christians may refer to as "working out your salvation." It calls for serving the needs of those who often are ignored or oppressed. At the conclusion of the parable of the Good Samaritan, Jesus asked the lawyer, "Which of these three, do you think, proved to be a neighbor to the man who fell among the robbers?" He said, "The one who showed mercy to him." And Jesus said to him, "Go and do the same" (Luke 10:36–37). It is quite clear that once we believe in Christ and claim the salvation that he brings, that we are to then extend forgiveness and service to others. Our salvation needs to be fleshed out through meeting the needs of others. In the profession of social work, needs are met through programs, advocacy, referrals, and counseling. Micah 6:8 (NIV) tells us, "To act justly and to love mercy and to walk humbly with your God." In social work practice, we show mercy and seek justice for all clients through providing services and resources to help clients succeed.

For the Christian social worker, the core values in the profession align with what Scripture calls us to do. We are called to show mercy and serve others. Social work serves all areas of needs ranging from illness, abuse, crime, poverty, addiction, and mental health. The field of social work provides a unique perspective on the doctrine of salvation because in many ways it does mirror the image of salvation. By helping clients restore well-being or reform a behavior, this provides a path for them to move forward with hope, which is the primary goal in all social work practice.

Related Scripture

John 1:9–18
John 3:3–21
Acts 4:11–12
Acts 16:25–34
Romans 10:5–17
Ephesians 2:1–10
Titus 3:3–7

===

FURTHER READING

Demarest, Bruce. *The Cross and Salvation: The Doctrine of Salvation*. Wheaton, IL: Crossway, 2006.

Holcomb, Justin S. *Christian Theologies of Salvation: A Comparative Introduction*. New York: New York University Press, 2017.

Packer, J. I. *Evangelism and the Sovereignty of God*. Downers Grove, IL: IVP, 1961.

Peterson, Robert. *Salvation Accomplished by the Son: The Work of Christ*. Wheaton, IL: Crossway, 2011.

Poe, Harry Lee. *The Gospel and Its Meaning*. Grand Rapids: Zondervan, 1996.

Schreiner, Thomas. *Faith Alone: The Doctrine of Justification: What the Reformers Taught . . . and Why It Still Matters*. Grand Rapids: Zondervan, 2015.

10

What the Church Is

American Christians—and evangelicals in particular—are not shy about talking about the church, what makes a good church, what the church does wrong, or what we want the church to do differently. Before we spend two chapters exploring the doctrine of the church, we need to be reminded of what the church really is.

We have all had friends get married, and if we are honest, we have had friends marry people that we have trouble getting along with. How does that impact your relationship with you and your friend? Have you said, "Hey, you know your fiancée? I really don't like to be around her?" What would happen if you did? How would your friend react? Prioritize the fiancée, right? You would expect that it would probably impact your friendship.

Let us reflect on a passage, Eph 5:22–32 (ESV). You have likely heard this passage before. It is an important passage in our understanding of the relationship between men and women, especially in the covenant of marriage. But let us look at it here for what it says to us about the church. In these verses, God says things like, "Husbands, love your wives, as Christ loved the church and gave himself up for her" (v. 25), and "husbands should love their wives as their own bodies" (v. 28). The relationship between Jesus Christ and the church is one of a sacrificial husband who loves and cherishes his wife!

I hope the illustration of your friend and his new wife is beginning to land. It can be tempting when we begin to talk about the doctrine of the church to drift toward ways that our own churches have failed us, or that we have been hurt by them, or ways that we do not really like them. We might be tempted at times to be among the crowd who say they love Jesus, but not the church. But as you just heard from Ephesians 5, to claim to love Jesus but not the church is just like claiming to still like your friend but hate the spouse. You know that would impact your relationship. When we are talking about the doctrine of ecclesiology, we must remember that we are speaking of the bride of our Savior. We must talk about the church in a way that is honest, but also honoring. If we are going to be true to the gospel, we must call out mistakes and abuses. But I want us to make sure that you do not take the easy route of just being an armchair critic of the church, as though you can just pick Jesus and not the church. Places like Ephesians 5 help us see why that is impossible. Jesus loves the church, Jesus died for the church, Jesus nourishes the church, and Jesus is perfecting the church.

BIBLICAL PICTURES OF THE CHURCH

How do we begin to think about the church? In these two chapters, we are going to talk about the marks of the church and then the function of the church. We will begin here with an exploration of the word "church" and the way it is pictured in the Bible.

What do we think of when we hear the phrase "the church," even the basic definition of the term? The Greek word translated "church" is *ecclesia*. This word was often used to refer to an assembly of citizens of a city. It literally means "called-out ones." In other words, the very word that God used in the New Testament means "the people gather." In Hebrew, the word translated into this same idea is *kahal*, which designates "assembling together." When we talk about the church, when we talk about the basic definition of the church, it is this idea of a people that is called together, assembled for the purpose of worshipping God.

The same word is used both for the universal church and the local church. The universal church is all believers in Christ at all times and in all places. The local church is a group of believers that meets in a specific geographical location with some sense of common membership. We know this because Paul talked about casting people out of the membership.

When the New Testament uses *ecclesia*, it primarily refers to local bodies of believers. This reality can help us prioritize the importance of the local church as the expression of church rather than the abstract, universal church. It is not just that the universal church is the body of Christ, and your local church is only a small replica. The New Testament says that the local church is the body of Christ too. We must recognize that there is a very high view of the local congregation in the New Testament. There is something about that local "coming together" that God chooses to use uniquely in the sanctification of his people and the work of Christ in the world.

God provides three pictures of the church in the Bible. The first is the "people of God." In 2 Cor 6:16, Paul wrote, "I will dwell and walk among them, and I will be their God, and they will be my people." This picture emphasizes God's initiative in choosing people. The church is the chosen people of God, and they belong to God. God belongs to them. We see the marks of this with circumcision in the Old Testament, and circumcision of the heart in the New Testament. This picture also reminds us that holiness is expected of the church. Purity and sanctification are key.

The second biblical picture of the church is the "body of Christ." This is the most extended image of the church in the New Testament. It emphasizes that the church is the focal point of Christ's activity now, just like his physical body was when he was on earth. This picture emphasizes the notion of believers in union with Christ. It is obvious that if you want to know what a person is doing, you look at that person. If you want to know what Jesus is doing in the world, where do you look? You look at his body, the church. (That is not to say God does not work outside the church. God works in *everything*. However, God sometimes works outside the church as a form of judgment against the unfaithfulness of the church. But what the New Testament makes clear, is that the church is the body of Christ.) The primary means for Christ's action in the world today is his body.

This idea of the body of Christ is used of the universal church, but it is also used of the local church. We see that Christ is the head of the body. The members are the individual parts. In the New Testament, the persons who make up the church are connected. There is no such thing as an isolated Christian. I often try to get the strangeness of the "Christian without the church" across to students with a little experiment:

> Let's all close our eyes. Imagine it was about forty minutes ago, and you were hustling to Jennings Hall to get to class on time. After walking across campus and hearing the bell tower, you reach Jennings, grab the door handle, and pull it open. As you look down, you notice there on the rug, just inside the door, a severed toe. How might you have responded forty minutes ago if you'd opened the door and seen a severed toe? I

probably would have been late to class. What else would you have thought? Whose toe is this? Where's the rest of the body? Maybe, if you know anything about severed toes, you might have had a moment of clarity where you thought, *I'll go find some ice!* You would have recognized, as soon as you opened that door and saw the toe on the ground, something was not right. Yet we don't think much about Christians who are not meaningfully connected to a local church.

When we draw out this image of the body of Christ, we realize that sanctification does not depend on being an individual, solo Christian. It depends on being part of a body because the body of Christ is what God uses by his Spirit to perfect us. It will not go any better for a severed Christian than it will for a severed toe.

The third biblical picture of the church is the "temple of the Holy Spirit." The Spirit brought the church into being. We see this first at Pentecost when the Holy Spirit descended as tongues of fire (Acts 2:3). The apostles then went out and preached, and thousands were added to their number. We also know from our exploration of the doctrine of salvation that it is the Spirit's work in us that turns us back to Christ. Our individual experiences of being united to the body of Christ are connected to the work of the Holy Spirit. The church is indwelled by the Spirit. First Corinthians 3:16 says that "you are God's temple" and "the Spirit of God lives in you." We often read verses like this one as written only to individuals, but the letter is addressed to an entire church, and the "you" here is a plural "you," closer to the Southern "y'all" than the singular, individualist "you." The Holy Spirit gives power to the church and brings unity to the church (Acts 4:32). The Holy Spirit is the means of Jesus's presence with the church; the Holy Spirit makes the church holy and pure. Since the church is filled with imperfect but being perfected humans, the church itself is on a road to perfection. The unity that Jesus desires for the church—which we will discuss momentarily—is something that we as humans cannot achieve on our own. It is something that we should long for and that we should pray for. We should certainly never sacrifice truth for the sake of unity because we can't be the one body of Christ if we sacrifice the truth of Christ. I'm not saying we should sacrifice truth for unity, but we should be people who long for unity and pray for unity and look forward to the day in eternity when that unity will be clear. Unity is one of the defining marks of what the church is supposed to be.

MARKS OF THE CHURCH

When it comes to what the church is supposed to be, or what we see as the church, we might desire to just go back to the New Testament and look at what the church was in the New Testament and seek to match up with it. But according to Gerald Bray, no church today can aspire to re-create the New Testament situation,[1] for several reasons. First, the New Testament has not given us enough details about how particular congregations were organized. Second, the apostles are no longer with us, and when we look at how churches were governed in the New Testament, they were always subject to being overruled by the apostles. In other words, the New Testament church existed in a unique situation in the history of redemption, where the apostles held unique authority given them by Jesus. Third, two thousand years of history have left their mark. We see things about the way church is done in the New Testament that is unique to that context. The church is now a worldwide phenomenon with a great deal of diversity. We see some diversity, even in the New Testament, but much more today.

If reconstructing New Testament church proves difficult, how do we take our cue from the New Testament? In other words, how do we make sure our understanding of the church fits with the New Testament, and is true to the New Testament without being limited only to the way it is described in the New Testament? How can we seek faithful expressions of church today? It is not that we can't know anything about the church from the New Testament; we can. But we are not given those exact blueprints, so whatever we're going to do, we do that by trying to honor what the New Testament reveals about the nature of the church.

The first way that we are going to talk about this and define the church is by exploring the four marks of the church. These four marks are drawn from early creeds: *one, holy, catholic,* and *apostolic.* What do these four pieces mean? As we explore these terms, we will see they define the existing church while also remaining ideals to which the church aspires.

---

[1] Gerald Bray, *The Church: A Theological and Historical Account* (Grand Rapids: Baker Academic, 2016), 222–23.

One

What does it mean to say that the church is one? On the one hand, we can see that this is true; the church is "one" in some big sense. But on the other hand, the church is not one at all! Even small towns tend to have more than one church, and often the divisions are clear. "One" seems flatly false because of our lived experiences of churches. Unity is something that is not as important to us as it should be. We are so used to disunity and disagreement. We do not value unity, but we should because Jesus does. If you look at the high priestly prayer in John 17, the night that Jesus was betrayed, we have this long prayer that Jesus prays. He prays for unity. He prays that we might be one, and he uses his unity with the Father as the example, which is quite profound. We have already explored the unity in the Trinity and how hard that is to grasp. At some level, that is the unity Jesus desires. This oneness of the church points out to us something good about the church, that there is some unity between all Christian churches. It reminds us that we should aspire to see this unity more fully.

However, this is not what we are getting at with the oneness of the church. "One" highlights the unity of the church around the gospel message. Earlier in church history, oneness was demonstrated in a different way, and that there was much more unity among churches before the Reformation and the Great Awakening.

"One" does not mean there is only one church you can go to. It does not mean one church gets everything. It points to the unity of the church, a unity that we can still see to some degree in large denominations, or in the Roman Catholic Church. They can remind us of what this unity can look like. We should, like Jesus, long for the day when the unity of the church will be more visible than it is today. Rather than celebrating our disunity in our diversity and difference among all the churches, this mark of the church does point to something true. It also reminds us that the church is not something that is perfect now. As we see in Ephesians 5, the church is something that Christ is working to perfect. When she is perfected, the church will be one.

Holy

The second mark is similar in that it is true to some degree, but we also experience its lack at times. Holy. You have probably met some *un*holy people at church. There may have been experiences at church when you did not think,

This is a holy group of people. Sometimes these are relatively trivial things. Sometimes they are very serious things. Holiness can be hard for us to associate with the church, with various scandals in the news.

What does it mean that Christians say that the church is holy? On the one hand, what this refers to is that the church is properly made up of saints. Not people who are perfect, but people who have been declared holy and are being made holy by Christ. In other words, just as sanctification is the process going on in the life of all believers, being made holy is what is going on in the life of the church. The church is holy because God is making the church holy.

While the imperfections that we see in various local churches might tempt us to think that the church is not holy at all, we must discipline ourselves to remember that, just as we individually are on our way toward holiness and the image of Christ by the work of the Spirit, so too are our communities of faith. The holiness of the church is something that is just like our own individual holiness. It is established by Christ's work and made perfect by the Spirit's work in sanctification. The oneness points to unity, the holiness points to the fact that it is composed of saints, people who are declared and made holy by God.

Catholic

The third mark is catholic. In some American contexts, this word causes confusion, because we typically use it to refer primarily to the Roman Catholic Church. In places like the Apostles' Creed, "catholic" is used in its older, fuller sense, which simply means "universal"; it means "applicable to all."

Our culture loves us and hates us for this mark. We are probably more used to seeing the positive side of this mark. The fact of the church's catholicity means the church is for everyone. There is no one to be excluded from the body of Christ based on their race, sex, or background. All those who trust in Christ as Savior are part of this one body. In a world that is increasingly divided—even if the lines of division change—this openness and universality is truly a light and a witness. Our culture currently appreciates this bent toward unity. The church is for everyone.

But why is it for everyone? The church is for everyone because, as it was said in the early church, "Outside the church, there is no salvation." That is incredibly offensive in our culture.

You might hear that and think, *Oh, that's not true. You don't have to go to church to get saved.* That is not the same. Remember, "church" here is a word that, as we will discuss more below, refers to the body of Christ. To be saved, especially in New Testament language, is to be "in Christ," as Paul so often puts it. When you are in Christ, you are in the body of Christ. "Outside the church, there is no salvation" means, theologically, that you cannot be saved without becoming part of the body of the Savior. It is not saying that must happen in a church building. Outside the church, there is no salvation because there is no salvation apart from being united with Christ. There is no salvation apart from becoming part of this body. That is part of what *catholic* means. That is offensive. Not only is the church open to all; everyone, everywhere, needs the church.

Apostolic

Last, the church is apostolic. This mark can also be a bit confusing. We can view it in a couple different ways. Some churches, such as the Roman Catholic Church, would say to be apostolic means that you can trace your leadership all the way back to the apostles. Protestant churches would typically say that a church bears the mark of the apostles, not by some line of leadership, but by a faithfulness to the apostles' teaching. In other words, "apostolic" is another way of talking about churches being centered on the gospel, the message of the apostles. The gospel message of the apostles is all-encompassing and requires discipleship and connection to all of life. Like the apostles, we should see the gospel as life-altering and not just eternity-altering.

A CHURCH ON THE WAY: OR, HOW TO ACCOUNT FOR SIN AND BROKENNESS IN THE BODY

The four marks of the church that were just discussed can strike us as obviously true or obviously false, depending on our previous experience of the church. How can we talk about "one" church when we experience so many denominations and conflicts within individual churches? What does it mean to say "holy" when so many have experienced such real pain at the hands of Christians, and often leaders, within churches? "Catholic" can be confusing, and "universal" might seem to rule out the very local distinctives of individual churches. Finally, apostolic can seem false too, especially if your church is part of a denomination that did not exist at the time of Martin Luther, let alone the apostles!

The first answer to this challenge is that these marks characterize not only certain (partial) elements of the church today, but they also characterize the direction that the church is headed. When we experience the sin of Christians in the church, we are reminded that the church is being drawn toward holiness, not that it has achieved it. (If we return to Ephesians 5, we see in verse 26 that Jesus loves the church and demonstrates that love by cleansing the church.) When the church fails to demonstrate one or more of the marks, we must remember this aspect.

The second answer is to remind ourselves that it is God who is working to sanctify the church. We see this dynamic in personal salvation as well. Because of faith in Christ, the sinner is saved because they are justified by Jesus's finished work on the cross. It is done. They are "saved" in a real and full sense. At the same time, God's Spirit works to sanctify, to make holy, to make "saved" real in increasingly full ways until the end, when believers are promised glorification (Rom 8:30). When we see sin in the life of the believer or in the life of the church, the right response is not rejecting that person or that church, but to remind ourselves that God is at work—while at the same time pointing that person or that church to the truth of the gospel to hold them to account. In other words, we do not give a free pass to sin in Christians or in the church. But God has revealed to us that this is a process, so we should not be surprised when we see evidence of how long of a process that can be. The church can sometimes be a house with clear problems, clear places that need attention and correction, by God's grace. But just like we would not tear down a house just because of a leaky roof, we don't discard the bride of Christ because of the blemishes that Christ is still working to cleanse.

CONCLUSION

Our discussion of the doctrine of the church must be rooted in the biblical pictures that God has given us. The church is the bride of Christ, and we should not flippantly think we can love Jesus and hate or demean his bride. The church is the people of God, the body of Christ, and the temple of the Holy Spirit (see page 130). The church is one, holy, catholic, and apostolic, in very real ways, but also in what God has promised to do in the life of Christians and in the life of the church.

One field of study that has frequently been connected to church life and church work is business. How can the insights of business scholars into the ins and outs of institutions help us think about what the church is, and what local churches are? To what degree does the Christian faith, and the doctrine of the church, push back against aspects of this field of study?

The Church as a Business Enterprise
RICHARD J. MARTINEZ, PHD

There seems a great distance between the study, understanding, and practice of business organizing and most discussions of the doctrine of the church. While the church as the body of Christ exists to perpetuate biblical unity, verity, and purity among its members, in the business arena, there is an omnipresent assumption that profit, or "making money," is the overarching reason for the enterprise to exist. And yet, allusions to mammon and "filthy lucre" aside, without the organizational mechanisms emerging from the business arena, the church would suffer greatly in pursuit of its divinely ordained mission.

As the mystery of the gospel plays out through the body of Christ and its various members, the mission and ministry of the church must be translated into pragmatic mechanisms. As such, the body of Christ takes on a physical, organizational form, just as the Son of Man took on a physical, human form. In this physical context, the church employs organizational, hierarchical, and even specific business elements.

If we shine our spotlight on the business elements of the church, we find the ever-present challenge of the physical form being in the world, but not of the world. Business and organizational processes are critical for the church on earth to fulfill its mission. It is helpful, therefore, to consider (very briefly) business elements that translate well into the church arena, and those which do not so translate.

Translatable Business Factors

In pursuit of the church's mission, we find ourselves in need of many of the principles and processes that make business organizations successful. For example, noting that the physical form of the church requires various forms of capital (not just financial) to operate, we find that (individual) churches go through the various stages of business development common to all organizations: including birth, growth, maturity, decline, and death. Along this trajectory, some of the translatable business elements are positive forces in achieving the effectiveness and efficiency necessary for organizations to thrive. Other business elements are negative forces in church organizations, just as they are in other types of enterprise.

On the positive side, we know that appropriate structuring maximizes church efficiency and facilitates good stewardship of scarce resources. That is not real interesting to most gospel-driven church servants, but it is necessary. At the same time, we know that, as a church grows, it can gain "economies of scale," which essentially means that larger organizations have lower costs of production per service provided, whatever that means in the church context. It might mean lower costs of supplies due to volume discounts. Or, almost tongue in cheek, it could mean lower "costs per baptism," as building, filling, and heating a baptismal font is the same whether we baptize one person or fifty. And four services on a weekend utilizing the same building is more efficient than holding one service in four separate, costly venues.

At the same time, many business marketing and entrepreneurship principles and processes have been adopted by church organizations as they seek to build, grow, and reposition for a changing culture and demographic. Market research principles—surveys, data analysis, focus groups—have helped churches understand their communities and populations, to better know how they might serve and minister to them, as well as how to speak gospel truth in a way that is best understood by the various generations. Entrepreneurial efforts have helped churches respond to the data and information generated by those marketing processes, and either plant new churches or modify existing church efforts to best represent Christ in ways that reflect his eternal truths to ever-changing demographics.

All of that said, not all business elements are positive. While businesses of all types benefit greatly from organizational and other business processes, they also struggle with the fallen nature of such processes. For example, all organizations, including churches, encounter group/team/staff dysfunctions, as well as some levels of toxicity in leadership and culture. While churches benefit from the business practice of strategic planning, they may also encounter drift and atrophy resulting from a loss of mission definition and focus. Further, as churches benefit from the gifts of strong servant leadership, they often falter in the cult of personality, or the identification of a church with a strong, charismatic leader whose persona displaces the centrality of Christ in the church. In general, like all organizations, churches encounter diseconomies of scale—wherein the benefits of size are offset by the liabilities of size—and mismanagement of resources, including finances, people, and facilities. Churches are in most ways better off in their physical form as they employ sound business and organizational principles but are in some ways also vulnerable to the pitfalls of business imperfections.

Non-Translatable Business Factors

It should be noted that some business aspects simply do not translate well to the physical church arena. For example, the default profit mentality of business is problematic as we seek to apply business principles to the church. As is true with most non-profit organizations, churches do not (should not) seek profit in the traditional business sense. Church resources above operating costs are thus expected to be utilized to advance the identified evangelical ministries of the congregation, not to enrich ecclesiastical participants. As such, it becomes critical for church leaders to identify and articulate the specific, Christ-centered, non-profit mission, vision, and goals of the congregation, so that achievement can be measured and adjusted as necessary. In the absence of profit or (primarily) monetary goals, the church as organization will suffer without more appropriate biblical targets.

Second, one of the driving forces of business thought and effort is market share and market power. Nonetheless, churches do not (should not) seek to "outdo" other churches for the sake of some zero-sum organizational competition. Rather, churches in the body of Christ cooperate to expand the kingdom, presumably at the expense of the enemy's "market share."

In the end, many of the questions that materialize when we consider application of business principles to the body of Christ are exacerbated as the size of the congregation transcends certain organizational boundaries. As the hipster coffee shop generates revenues that might be marked for outreach or missions, and the church "Resource Center" or "Gift Shop" features the worship band's latest CD, is it possible to maintain the centrality of Christ's gospel in the mindset of the church? Churches cannot grow beyond a certain point without utilizing business-organizing principles—and being tempted by more profit-oriented business principles. It is a fine line, and not always easy to recognize as church leaders pursue the gospel mission of the church amid the business-organizing processes that make the pursuit possible.

Related Scripture

Matthew 16:13–20
Romans 12:3–8, 12–26
Ephesians 2:11–22
Ephesians 5:22–32
1 Peter 2:1–12
Revelation 21:1–8

FURTHER READING

Allison, Gregg. *Sojourners and Strangers: The Doctrine of the Church*. Wheaton, IL: Crossway, 2012.

Clowney, Edmund. *The Church*. Downers Grove, IL: IVP, 1995.

Gohenn, Michael. *Light to the Nations: The Missional Church and the Biblical Story*. Grand Rapids: Baker Academic, 2011.

Hammett, John. *Biblical Foundations for Baptist Churches: A Contemporary Ecclesiology*, 2nd edition. Grand Rapids: Kregel, 2019.

Harper, Brad, and Paul Louis Metzger. *Exploring Ecclesiology: An Evangelical and Ecumenical Introduction*. Grand Rapids: Brazos, 2009.

Husbands, Mark, and Daniel Treier. *The Community of the Word: Toward an Evangelical Ecclesiology*. Downers Grove, IL: IVP, 2005.

Leeman, Jonathan. *Political Church: The Local Assembly as Embassy of Christ's Rule.* Downers Grove, IL: IVP Academic, 2016.

Minear, Paul S. *Images of the Church in the New Testament.* Louisville: Westminster John Knox, 2004.

11

What the Church Does

Now that we've covered what the church *is* by exploring the marks of the church, we can turn to what the church *does*. On one hand, this seems obvious: the church worships. On the other hand, it seems quite complex: different churches devote themselves to very different and sometimes contradictory activities. How do we know what the church is supposed to do?

One simple way to describe what the church does flows from the idea of the church as the body of Christ (Rom 12:5; 1 Cor 12:12–27; Eph 3:6; 5:23; Col 1:18, 24). The church carries out Christ's ministry in the world today. That ministry is tied to the ministry that Jesus himself conducted while on earth: spreading the news (in word and in deed) of the coming of the kingdom of God. This coming kingdom is brought about through the gospel, the good news, that the church preaches about Jesus. This gospel centers on the truths that Jesus is fully God and fully human, he died for the sins of the world, was buried, rose again, appeared to many, ascended into heaven, and will come again.

The apostles formed the church filled with believers who were charged to be Christ's body by spreading this message, by pointing to its reality in their words and actions. The church's job is to bear witness to the gospel. This witness takes many forms, but four are central: *the witness of evangelism*, *the witness of works of mercy*, *the witness of edification*, and *the witness of worship*.

WITNESS 1: EVANGELISM

The first activity that the church does in bearing witness to the gospel as the body of Christ is evangelism. In short, evangelism is bearing witness to the truth of the gospel through words: telling the world about the gospel.

Jesus commanded his disciples to do this. Following are two examples. First, in Acts 1:8 we read, "But you will receive power when the Holy Spirit comes on you; and you will be my witnesses in Jerusalem, and in all Judea and Samaria, and to the ends of the earth" (NIV). Jesus's words are quite clear: the disciples are to bear witness about him and his work after he leaves and sends the Holy Spirit to empower them. This statement makes clear that being witnesses is the main thing that followers of Jesus were to do, and it also demonstrates that what the church is supposed to do is not done under its own power, but in the power of the Holy Spirit. While we are looking at four different actions that the church does that can be understood as forms of witness, it is most likely that this verse refers to the most obvious, straightforward form of witness: using words to tell the truth of the gospel to those who have not heard. This is the primary action of the church. And this action is aimed indiscriminately outward. The progression that Jesus uses utilizes some categories that his disciples would have been familiar with (the regions Judea and Samaria), but the geographical progression is obvious: it goes out from Jerusalem to the ends of the earth. Likewise, Christians today can obey this command by beginning to speak the truth of the gospel right where they are, and pushing that message out without boundaries: everyone, all nations, need to hear it.

We see a more detailed example in Matt 28:16–20 (NIV):

> Then the eleven disciples went to Galilee, to the mountain where Jesus had told them to go. When they saw him, they worshiped him; but some doubted. Then Jesus came to them and said, "All authority in heaven and on earth has been given to me. Therefore go and make disciples of all nations, baptizing them in the name of the Father and of the Son and of the Holy Spirit, and teaching them to obey everything I have commanded you. And surely I am with you always, to the very end of the age."

We see two important pieces here as the verse expands on two aspects of what making more disciples means. First, they are to "baptize them." This statement of course does not mean to forcefully dunk people into nearby bodies of water or to sprinkle water on heads in the marketplace; rather "baptizing" here assumes the previous part of the pair that we see throughout the New Testament: repent. So, the first part of making disciples involves telling people the truth of the gospel so that they might repent, believe, and be baptized. (The second important piece, "teaching them to obey," will come into play below under the third form of witness.)

The most obvious form of witness, evangelism is a vital issue of obedience to the last words of Jesus before his ascension. The body of Christ is supposed to speak the truth of the gospel, of the world's need for salvation through faith in Jesus Christ. The disciples—and by extension, all disciples—were to take the gospel message everywhere, to all nations, to every type of people. They were to spread this message with their words. But this is not the only way that the church can bear witness to the gospel. We can point to it with more than our words.

WITNESS 2: WORKS OF MERCY

The second form that the church's witness takes is through good deeds done for others. These actions are often taken for granted when we think of the church: the church should help the poor, be positive influences in their communities, and make a difference in the world. We see ideas like this in the Old Testament in such verses as Mic 6:8 (ESV), which says, "He has told you, O man, what is good; and what does the LORD require of you but to do justice, and to love kindness, and to walk humbly with your God?" Here we see the notions of justice, kindness, and humility, characteristics of good actions that God's people are to do. At one level, the church should do these actions simply because they characterize God's people. But we can go deeper than that as well.

The New Testament is filled with similar ideas, including the works of Jesus and the writings of the apostles to believers. For example, James wrote, "Religion that God our Father accepts as pure and faultless is this: to look after orphans and widows in their distress and to keep oneself from being polluted by the world" (Jas 1:27 NIV). Here James gives looking after orphans and widows on the same level as avoiding worldly pollution and sin as defining pure and faultless religion. It seems simple and straightforward.

But how do verses like these, which clearly command good deeds, relate to the church's job to be witnesses to the gospel, to the coming kingdom of God? Making this connection clear is vital to seeing the unity of what the church is to do. In many circles, Christians feel a tension between evangelism and being concerned with social issues. They feel like there must be some choice between sharing words of the gospel and meeting the needs of people. That simply doesn't need to be the case. It is clear that both can happen, and both can be important.

There is more to it than this relationship between words and works, however. It is not only that the words of the church about the gospel and the works of mercy that the church is supposed to carry out do not need to compete; in fact, these both find their completion as forms of witness. Both point to the truth of the gospel, the good news that the kingdom of God is coming, and Jesus has provided a way into it for those who have faith in them. We can think of it this way: the words of the church point to the truth of the gospel explicitly; what Christians say in evangelism makes the gospel clear. But this message that God's kingdom has come in Jesus does not often fit with what goes on around us. We see much brokenness and pain in the world. The works of mercy, then, point to the reality of the gospel as well by making it real in small ways.

Works of mercy are not isolated actions but integrated with evangelism. The church says the kingdom is coming, and then the church shows what the kingdom is like. The church does not only help the orphan because of the command in James; the church helps the orphan because there are no orphans in God's kingdom. The church does not clothe the naked and feed the hungry only because nakedness and hunger are problems, but because the church proclaims a kingdom where there will be no more suffering. These actions bear witness to the truth of the gospel by being small but very real pictures of the kingdom Jesus brings.

Christian churches and other organizations are often part of the first response to natural disasters and other needs in the broken world. This is something Christians should realize is not separate from the gospel-proclamation work of evangelism. The purpose of this work, rightly understood, should be to point to the same gospel that we proclaim with our words. We cannot assume that the world will understand that connection, so we should still make it with our words. But we must realize that works of mercy do in fact point to the gospel. Christians are not simply being nice; they're showing what Jesus's kingdom looks like.

WITNESS 3: EDIFICATION

To begin to understand this third form the church's witness can take—edification—we must return to a previous point. When we reviewed Matt 28:16–20 above, we noted two ways that the disciples were to make more disciples: through conversion/baptism, and then through teaching those disciples to obey Jesus's commands. Teaching others to obey is a form of building one another up, of edification. The third activity the church does to bear witness to the gospel is to build one another up in the truths of the gospel, in the teachings of Jesus. The church is to build one another up to say and do what we are to say and do.

We see this elsewhere in the New Testament, of course. For example, Paul urges Timothy, "Preach the word; be ready in season and out of season; correct, rebuke, and encourage with great patience and teaching" (2 Tim 4:2). This advice is an expansion and explanation of what it means to teach disciples to obey, to build one another up. The center of preaching the word was preaching the gospel, of bearing witness to it, in order to help believers grow. So not only does the church tell the unbelieving world about the gospel through evangelism; the church also points to the truth of the gospel and its implications for itself, building up the body.

One more example from Paul. In Eph 4:11–13, Paul explains God's gifts of ministry to the believers. He says, "So Christ himself gave the apostles, the prophets, the evangelists, the pastors and teachers, to equip his people for works of service, so that the body of Christ may be built up until we all reach unity in the faith and in the knowledge of the Son of God and become mature, attaining to the whole measure of the fullness of Christ" (NIV). In these verses we see more about the purpose of this edification. Edification does not only mean instruction in what to think and believe, but also preparation for "works of service." These works themselves are also aimed at the body of Christ, that it might be built up in unity and maturity. The gifts that God gives the church are to build up the church, to bring the believers to maturity in what they believe, say, and do.

In this explanation of edification as building up the body, we find an interesting parallel. Another picture of the church in the New Testament is that of a temple (1 Cor 3:16; see page 130). So, we could shift our picture a bit here and say that God gives gifts to believers to build his temple. This should remind us of the way God worked in the Old Testament: he equipped Bezalel to be able to do what needed to be done to build the tabernacle in the wilderness, the traveling temple of sorts. Recall the tabernacle: it was to include many items that required skill to produce. While we might expect Moses to survey his people for the requisite skills, we see something different. We read, "Then the LORD said to Moses, 'See, I have chosen Bezalel son of Uri, the son of Hur, of the tribe of Judah, and I have filled him with the Spirit of God, with wisdom, with understanding, with knowledge and with all kinds of skills—to make artistic designs for work in gold, silver and bronze, to cut and set stones, to work in wood, and to engage in all kinds of crafts. Moreover, I have appointed Oholiab son of Ahisamak, of the tribe of Dan, to help him'" (Exod 31:1–6 NIV). God gave them the necessary skills to build the tabernacle, and gave them the ability to teach others (35:30–35) who also helped (36:1–2). We see a progression here: God gave the Holy Spirit so Bezalel had skills he would not otherwise have had; he used those skills to teach others. Together they built the tabernacle. In short, God equipped Bezalel to build up, to "edify" the tabernacle.

Just as God sent his Spirit in the Old Testament to build his tabernacle, he also distributes gifts to the church, through the Spirit, for the purpose of building his temple, the church. Edification is a form of bearing witness to the gospel, as the truth of the gospel brings unity and maturity in word and in deed. The church itself stands as witness to the truth of the gospel; edification builds up the church and sends out people to do the other forms of witness as well. In a way, this third form of witness is the church bearing witness to one another, reminding one another of the truth of the gospel and teaching them to bear witness. But there is one more form of witness to consider.

WITNESS 4: WORSHIP

The last form that the church's witness takes is worship. Now, of the four, this one might seem like the biggest stretch. How does worship relate to bearing witness to the truth of the gospel? In this way: if evangelism is bearing witness with words to the world, works of mercy are ways of bearing witness to the world with deeds, and edification is a way of bearing witness to one another and building one another up, then we can talk about worship as a way of bearing witness to God, praising him for who he is and what he has done in Jesus Christ.

Another issue to address right away is that worship is more than simply the musical aspect of the worship service, or even the worship service itself. While we want to acknowledge that is true—all of life should be worship for the follower of Christ—it is also helpful to think about what the purpose of the worship gathering is. Why has the church always both gathered and worshiped God in their individual, day-to-day lives?

In both the Old and New Testament, God's people have praised him in song. We see this in such books as the Psalms as well as in references in the New Testament. For instance, Paul wrote, "Instead, be filled with the Spirit, speaking to one another with psalms, hymns, and songs from the Spirit. Sing and make music from your heart to the Lord, always giving thanks to God the Father for everything, in the name of our Lord Jesus Christ" (Eph 5:18–20 NIV). The church has met together to sing praises to God, to pray, and to hear the Word of God preached. (Another element of the worship service is the Lord's Supper, which we will deal with in the next section.) From early on, Christian leaders encouraged believers not to neglect this meeting together (Heb 10:25).

Now that we have explained the four main actions that the church does as forms of "witness," we must consider how they relate together. Traditionally, the church has gathered to participate together in the third and fourth forms of witness (edification and worship), and they have done the other two activities when they were scattered out from the worship service. They did not do their evangelism and works of mercy in the weekly worship gathering. The weekly worship gathering was for edification and worship. Today, churches disagree on this balance, and some emphasize evangelism in the worship gathering to such a degree that not much edification (spiritual growth) or worship really takes place. So even as we understand these four forms that witness takes in the life of the church, we must think carefully about how the church remains faithful to each.

Finally, one more word on witness. Relating all four of these to the idea of "witness" helps us avoid some traps. Others think of witnessing only as evangelism, sharing the truth of the gospel with someone who does not yet believe. This section has demonstrated that the various activities of the church do find their justification in spreading the gospel, but they bear witness to the gospel in different ways. The church must guard against missing any of these elements, for the gospel is truly good news, and the church must point to it, bearing witness to the world, to itself, and to God of the good news of this message.

Now that we have considered the four main actions of the church, we must look more specifically at some actions that typically happen within a worship service and may seem difficult to connect to this idea of the church's task of witness. They are the ordinances: baptism and the Lord's Supper.

ORDINANCES

We cannot finish talking about what the church does without explaining the two other actions that Jesus commanded the church to do (besides making disciples): baptism and the Lord's Supper. The term *ordinances* fits best because Jesus ordained or commanded that the church should practice them. Other denominations use the language of sacraments, and there are obviously differences on their practice and meaning. Instead of getting into that level of detail in this treatment, we will explore an overarching framework for understanding both baptism and the Lord's Supper and how they relate to everything else that the church does.

In short, both baptism and the Lord's Supper provide pictures of the gospel. They point to its truth by being visible reminders of different aspects of the gospel. Baptism is the picture that teaches us about what it means to become a child of God, and the Lord's Supper is the picture that helps us understand how we have the strength to continue in (and as) the body of Christ.

Baptism

Baptism provides a picture that teaches us what it means to become part of God's people. It is the act of immersing the new believer in water and then bringing them up out of the water. This was the earliest way that Christians performed baptism of new believers, though later the practice developed other ways as well, including sprinkling or pouring water.

Paul expressed the logic of baptism in Rom 6:4: "Therefore we were buried with him by baptism into death, in order that, just as Christ was raised from the dead by the glory of the Father, so we too may walk in newness of life." Baptism is a picture of this idea of new life, which the gospel provides, though it does not save on its own. In the New Testament, the disciples urged people to repent and be baptized (Acts 2:37), and other times baptism is mentioned alone as providing salvation (Mark 16:16; John 3:5; 1 Pet 3:21). As we noted above, however, it is most likely that "baptism" came to stand for the repentance and faith that come before baptism. It is a sign of the new covenant that God provides through Jesus.

The act of baptism points to the gospel by being a clear picture of the new life that the new believer has by virtue of faith in the gospel. Baptism is a public act, declaring to the world a new spiritual reality and calling them to it as well.

In addition, baptism speaks to the church as well—each new baptism reminds believers of their baptism and calls them back to live in light of it. So, if we return to our earlier forms of witness, baptism pictures the gospel to the world and to the church, playing a role in evangelism and edification.

Lord's Supper

While baptism provides a picture of what it means to be born again into God's people, the Lord's Supper provides a picture of what it means to continue in the life of faith with the people of God. The Lord's Supper is practiced differently in various Christian denominations, and even differently within denominations. Instead of focusing on these differences, we'll trace the biblical origins of this practice of breaking bread together.

Jesus shared a last meal with his disciples, and each of the Gospels recounts it (Matt 26:17–30; Mark 14:12–26; Luke 22:7–39; John 13:1–17:26). This meal included Jesus washing the disciples' feet to demonstrate servanthood (John 13:1–7) and Jesus stating that one of the disciples would betray him and sending Judas away (Matt 26:21–25). The center of the meal, however, took a form that the disciples likely would not have expected. This last meal was in the time of Passover; it was a Passover meal. Before we can understand how Jesus changed this meal, we must look back and see what sort of meal it was meant to be in the first place.

The meal that Jesus and his disciples were celebrating traces back to the time when God saved his people out of slavery in Egypt. God sent Moses to tell Pharaoh to let the people go, and Pharaoh resisted. God sent nine plagues, but Pharaoh continued to stubbornly refuse. The tenth plague was to result in the death of all the firstborn in the land. God commanded the Israelites to sacrifice a lamb to redeem their firstborn, to rub its blood on their doorposts, and to eat the cooked meat. After this plague, Pharaoh commanded the Israelites to leave immediately. And they did (Exodus 11).

The Israelites were to continue to have this Passover meal to remember the way that God saved them out of Egypt with a mighty hand because of his covenant with Abraham. In Exod 12:25–27 we read, "When you enter the land that the LORD will give you as he promised, you are to observe this ceremony. When your children ask you, 'What does this ceremony mean to you?' you are to reply, 'It is the Passover sacrifice to the LORD, for he passed over the houses of the Israelites in Egypt when he struck the Egyptians, and he spared our homes.'" In other words, the meal was to be observed to *remember*, and each element of the meal took on a special meaning to remind the people of an aspect of what happened. For instance, the unleavened bread reminded them of the haste in which they left (they did not have time for the bread to rise); the lamb reminded them of the sacrifice, and the bitter herbs reminded them of the difficulty and suffering. Each piece had a purpose as this meal reminded God's people of the salvation God brought.

Now we are ready to see how Jesus changed this meal. Matthew explains it this way: "As they were eating, Jesus took bread, blessed and broke it, gave it to his disciples, and said, 'Take and eat it; this is my body.' Then he took a cup, and after giving thanks, he gave it to them and said, 'Drink from it, all of you. For this is my blood of the covenant, which is poured out for many for the forgiveness of sins. But I tell you, I will not drink from this fruit of the vine from now on until that day when I drink it new with you in my Father's kingdom'" (Matt 26:26–29). What we see is that Jesus takes a meal infused with meaning, and he tweaks that meaning by changing what the items mean. The bread is his body, the wine, his blood. Just as the Passover meal was meant to remind God's people of his provision of salvation out of physical slavery in Egypt, so the Last Supper is meant to remind God's people of his provision of salvation out of spiritual slavery through Jesus's death on the cross. In the story recorded in Luke 22:19, Jesus explicitly says, "Do this in remembrance of me." The disciples were to continue this ritual meal, but with different meaning pointing to the new covenant.

We know that the early church practiced this meal because the apostles wrote about how to do it properly. Paul explained in 1 Cor 11:23–26 how the believers were to continue this practice. Here we see the same practice, with an additional purpose added. Not only did Paul repeat the element about remembering Jesus; he added that whenever the believers eat the bread and drink the cup, they are proclaiming the Lord's death until he comes. In other words, practicing the Lord's Supper is a way for the church to bear witness to the gospel, remembering it and reminding one another of it. This practice fits in with both the witness of evangelism and the witness of edification.

This treatment of the ordinances has not been extensive, and we've left out some things that divide Christians by their disagreement. Mostly this is because such explanations would require us to expand this chapter into several more, or into several books, or several sets of books. This explanation has attempted to make sense of the essence of the ordinances and rooting them in the witness that the church bears, pointing to the gospel.

SUMMARY OF WHAT THE CHURCH DOES

We have covered a lot of ground trying to explain what the church is supposed to do. Admittedly, we have not talked about everything a particular church might discern to be part of their calling as the body of Christ. Instead, we focused on the role of the church as the body of Christ to do Christ's work on earth, to bear witness to the coming of his kingdom. This witness takes four main forms: evangelism, works of mercy, edification, and worship. Each of these bears witness to the truth of the gospel in a different way, and they reinforce one another.

The two ordinances that the church practices—baptism and the Lord's Supper—are pictures that God gives to further bear witness to the story of the gospel, the story in which the church finds itself playing a key role. When new believers are baptized, we see a picture of the new spiritual birth receiving the mark of the new covenant. When believers take the Lord's Supper together, they remember Jesus's death together and proclaim its significance, looking forward expectantly to his return. All that the church does is rightly centered on this gospel, whether words spoken, deeds done, lessons taught, songs sung, or ordinances performed.

The Church and Political Science
MICAH J. WATSON

How does the doctrine of the church (and in particular, what the church does) challenge particular issues, practices, or assumptions in your field of study?

The doctrine of the church, and what the church does, challenges political science insofar as it assumes an alternative polis and potentially rival claims of a higher citizenship. Sunday morning after Sunday morning, and at events throughout the week, through the church God *forms* Christians through practices, preaching/teaching, fellowship, and the ordinances of baptism and communion. The church challenges the field of politics in a few ways; following are two.

First, the study of politics includes defining and measuring the use of power and the substance and boundaries of sovereignty. This is fine so far as it goes, but it is incomplete. Stalin's quip "How many divisions does the pope have?" in response to a question about getting help from the Vatican, illustrates an overly materialistic focus on measurable power and human sovereignty that characterizes much of political science. The church reminds us through ordinary and extraordinary events that there is more to the world and world events than what we can measure or what is written down in human law. It is good for us to recognize the secondary sovereignty that nations and governing authorities hold so long as we remember that God is the ultimate sovereign, and the "great events" that roil politics locally and globally do not surprise him nor thwart his plans. Every time we practice communion, we proclaim the Lord's death until he comes again. That he is Lord of lords and King of kings is not just window dressing but a strong political claim about where ultimate sovereignty lies. The Romans were right to see Jesus as a threat, even if his kingdom was different. The church can and should remind those of us who study political science of these truths.

Second, the contemporary study of politics includes a heavy to sometimes almost exclusive emphasis on various loci of personal identity, whether class, race, gender, or sexual orientation. This is not just politics, of course, but would also include some sociology, the various "critical studies," and to some extent disciplines like psychology and history. Those lenses can be helpful and appropriate for learning and understanding political and social dynamics, but at the same time, if elevated to ultimately define who human beings are, they can become totalizing and harmful. Week after week we gather to praise God and by doing so are reminded that our primary identity is in Christ and not these important but secondary identities. This truth should not be a shield with which to put off hard conversations about injustice, but rather a healthy church will prefigure the Revelation promise that "from every nation" God will call his people to him, and our common identity in Christ can ground healthy diversity and relationships with men and women, different races, and so on.

How does your field of study provide a unique perspective or way of thinking that can help Christians better understand this doctrine or related topics?

This is a tougher question, and I have struggled a bit with how to answer it. Much depends on how broad the "this doctrine or related topics" is. These two observations apply more to how Christians operate "out in the world" than they might to the internal warp and woof of daily and weekly life in our congregations.

First, Christians are called by God to care about justice. Jesus's parable of the sheep and the goats as well as the book of James make it clear that if we are faithful, we will act on that in the here and now with regard to the poor and the downtrodden. That message is clear in both the Old and New Testaments. God in his wisdom, however, did not leave us a detailed "how to" plan to put that call into action. While the OT tells us to leave out gleanings given the agricultural realities of that day, it is less clear what means are efficacious today on the local, state, national, and global level. Political science as a discipline employs analytical social science tools that can help us both identify the most important areas of need and measure the efficacy of our efforts. For example, Gary Haugen and his team at International Justice Mission (IJM) are motivated by their Christian convictions to fight against sex trafficking, land and property theft, and other injustices that run rampant in developing countries that do not have a robust rule-of-law regime. Their motivation is admirable, but motivation and good intentions alone are not enough. When we make a plan, we must count the cost, and political science (and other social sciences like economics) provide a more generalizable picture of what's happening beyond the mere anecdote. And so IJM can marshal arguments by using the insights of social science about the relationships between global aid spending and local law enforcement, about the realities of slavery in India despite it being technically against the law, and about the travesty that is the global sex trafficking industry given the toxic blend of sexual lust and economic greed that fuels it. Given God has called the church to care and act for justice, political science offers some tools that will help us answer that call with our minds as well as our hearts.

Second, Christians are called to share the gospel throughout the world. Once again good intentions are not enough. Sharing the gospel well means understanding the systems and cultures into which we are sending our missionaries. Political science is not the only discipline that fosters cultural awareness, but it is one important discipline that does so on the national, legal, and social level. In political science and in other disciplines there is often talk of "decentering" ourselves and our students. This can be salutary depending on what we are centering ourselves on and what is being displaced. While there is nothing wrong, and much right, with a godly appreciation of where God has planted us nationally in his sovereignty (i.e., there is such a thing as healthy patriotism), political science can help us understand other peoples and their ways of life such that we can attempt to distinguish what is culturally contingent in who we are and what is central to the gospel that we want to share. This is a tricky business for missionaries and too often we in the West have blurred the lines between what is Western and what is Christian. The perspectival lens that informs the comparativist subdiscipline of political science, properly understood, can help the church better equip its missionaries and preach the gospel well (sociology and anthropology could be added here too).

Related Scripture

Matthew 6:33
Matthew 4:17
Acts 2:37–41
1 Corinthians 11:23–34
1 Corinthians 12:13
1 Corinthians 14:26
Ephesians 4:11–12, 17–32
Ephesians 5:15–20
Titus 3:1–2

FURTHER READING

Allison, Gregg R. *Sojourners and Strangers: The Doctrine of the Church*. Downers Grove, IL: Crossway, 2012.

Bray, Gerald. *The Church: A Theological and Historical Account*. Grand Rapids: Baker, 2016.

Carson, D. A. *The Church in the Bible and the World*. Grand Rapids: Baker, 1987.

Easley, Kendell H. and Christopher W. Morgan. *The Community of Jesus: A Theology of the Church*. Nashville: B&H, 2013.

Smith, Gordon T. *Evangelical, Sacramental, and Pentecostal: Why the Church Should Be All Three*. Downers Grove, IL: IVP Academic, 2017.

12

Last Things

E schatology is meant to be a source of hope for the Christian life. That might come as a surprise to you. Especially in American evangelical Christianity, many people are first exposed to questions about the end times through books or films that promote a particular way of understanding the book of Revelation to confront people with the importance—indeed, the eternal significance—of faith in Christ. On one hand, these films are a good thing—too many people go through life without thinking about eternity at all. On the other hand, these films can promote misplaced fear among Christians. However you interpret the book of Revelation as a believer, the result should not be fear!

If we stop and think about the role that apocalyptic literature is supposed to play, we will see why. In Revelation, John was writing to persecuted Christians to encourage them to continue in their faith, standing strong no matter what opposition they faced or how bad things looked. Apocalyptic literature peels back appearances to make clear what is really going on. And in Revelation, we see that what is really going on is that God is in complete and utter control, guiding the affairs of people and the world to the end he planned for all along. This was written to encourage Christians, not to cause fear. Those who are in Christ, who belong to the Lamb, are assured of his ultimate victory and their unity with him.

INDIVIDUAL ENDS

Often when we think of eschatology, we jump immediately to questions about the end of the world. Any discussion of eschatology would be incomplete without exploring what the Bible reveals about that topic, but eschatology includes more than that. Under this doctrine we not only consider what happens at the end of all things, but also what happens at the end of individual lives.[1] What is the individual "experience" of the end? Or, perhaps more common: "What happens when someone dies?"

Our culture often denies the reality of death or tries to remove that reality from interrupting our lives. In earlier time periods, people could not ignore death: life expectancy was much lower, child mortality was much higher, and all of that dying was happening in the context of the home and community. Now, death happens more commonly in the contexts of institutions or accidents, removed from "normal life." This extends beyond human death too: We buy our meat already packaged in supermarkets. We do not see death as often, so we can ignore it more easily.

Furthermore, some futurists and technologists claim that death is something we can overcome altogether. In this way of thinking, the body is something like a "meat suit," something that we can hope to exchange for a more durable, longer-lasting outfit. We must remember that when death comes we are talking about the death of the body as a result of sin, and it is something that is real and something that is inevitable because of sin, and because death is a consequence of sin. Only Christ can overcome and redeem us from sin. It is only in Christ that death will be overcome, not through our own technological efforts. Death is real, and there is no escape. We can delay it in some cases, but we cannot and should not deny it.

Next, Scripture speaks of death as the separation of the body and the spirit (Jas 2:26). Death is not non-existence, but the separation of the spirit from the body when the body undergoes physical death. As we know from our understanding of the doctrine of humanity, humans are created as embodied souls, so this physical death of the body and separation of the soul cuts at the heart of what it means to be human. To be human is to be this unit, the strange unity of body and soul or spirit and flesh. Physical death, the result of sin, is the breaking of that bond. This is important for us to remember.

The separation of the spirit from the body is not something that is trivial. Even as we recognize the reality of death, we must remember that the nature of death points to the fact that it is a result of sin. It is an enemy, but it is a

---

[1] I rely on Millard Erickson in this approach because I think it is wise and helpful for students. He includes chapters on "Introductory Matters and Individual Eschatology," "The Second Coming and Its Consequents," "Millennial and Tribulational Views," and "Final States" in his part on the Last Things. See Erickson, *Introducing Christian Doctrine*, chapters 39–42.

conquered enemy. Physical death is not part of the original plan for humans. When death happens, it reminds us of the fall, and it is proper to rage against death. It is proper to mourn.

Once this separation occurs, what happens to the person? What do they experience? This is what is referred to as the intermediate state. There are a couple different viewpoints here that Christians hold. One option is called soul sleep. The position of soul sleep is that in between physical, personal death and Christ's return and bodily resurrection, it is just like sleeping. In other words, there is no conscious existence in between those two times. At Christ's return, the dead wake up. This position is drawn from various Bible passages that mention sleep in reference to death (Acts 7:60 does this; 13:36 and 1 Thessalonians 4 has similar language). Soul sleep also emphasizes that the person is a unitary element, an embodied soul or a soulful body. When the body stops functioning, the person, at some level ceases to consciously exist, according to soul sleep.

You may be anticipating some objections to this view. For instance, Scripture says that when you are absent from the body we are present with the Lord (2 Cor 5:8). There is also the parable that Jesus tells of the Rich Man and Lazarus (Luke 16:19–31), which builds on the notion of conscious existence after death and before resurrection.

Another position emphasizes what Paul wrote in 2 Cor 5:8: "To be absent from the body and to be present with the Lord" (NKJV). According to this position, when people die, they experience the presence of Christ if they are united with Christ through faith, or they experience his absence and await judgment if they are not believers. While many people label these ideas with "heaven" or "hell," it is important to note that Scripture teaches that there is a difference between the intermediate state (what happens to people between death and final judgment) and the eternal state (what happens to people after final judgment). We will discuss this more momentarily, but at this stage it is important to note that there is a difference between these "places." Those who die "in Christ" experience his presence and await the final judgment and their eternal life with God.

The next piece that Christians agree on in relation to individual eschatology begins to connect with cosmic eschatology. Christians believe that Jesus will come again. We do not know the time, but we know that he is coming back. This is one of the most clearly taught doctrines in the entire New Testament.

This second coming of Christ is personal. It will be the actual person of Christ who returns, the Second Person of the Trinity who took on flesh and ascended into heaven. As the angels put it to the disciples when Jesus ascended into heaven: "This same Jesus . . . will come in the same way that you have seen him going into heaven" (Acts 1:11). He will return triumphantly, with great power and glory (Matt 24:30). When Christians talk about Jesus's return as being "soon," we do not mean that we know exactly when it will be, but we trust that it is the next major step in God's plan, and everything is set for it to happen. Christ's return serves as a helpful point to cross over from "individual eschatology" to "cosmic eschatology," or the end of all things, as his return ushers in this stage for all creation. Individuals will experience cosmic eschatology; the distinction is meant to help us see divisions between questions about what Christians should expect after personal death (individual eschatology) and what Christians believe about the end of all things (cosmic eschatology).

THE END OF ALL THINGS

The end of all things begins with the return of Jesus Christ, which is related to several key ideas that we need to understand. We will discuss the millennial reign of Christ, the rapture, the final judgment, and then eternity.

Christians believe in the millennial reign of Christ because Scripture speaks about it. This belief is based most clearly on Rev 20:4: "Then I saw thrones, and people seated on them who were given authority to judge. I also saw the souls of those who had been beheaded because of their testimony about Jesus and because of the word of God, who had not worshiped the beast or his image, and who had not accepted the mark on their foreheads or their hands. They came to life and reigned with Christ for a thousand years."

While Christians agree that there is a doctrine of the millennium, disagreement emerges based on the interpretation of two ideas: "reigned with Christ" and "thousand years." Three classic positions differ in their expectations regarding these parts of Rev 20:4. They are: premillennialism, postmillennialism, and amillennialism.

Premillennialism holds that Christ will return and then reign on the earth for a literal 1,000-year period along with believers. At the end of this time, Satan will be let loose, rebelling and suffering final defeat. After this defeat, Christ will judge, condemning Satan and the wicked to eternal punishment. After this judgment, the eternal states—how people will exist for eternity—begin.

Postmillennialism holds that Christ will return after peace and righteousness reign on earth. This view expects the elimination of war and other evils, the existence of Christian governments, and mass conversion to Christianity. Many hold to this being a literal 1,000 years as well, though others interpret this time as symbolic. This period is followed by Christ's return, one general resurrection of the dead, one judgment, and then the eternal states.

Amillennialism does not interpret the 1,000 years of Revelation 20:4 as literal calendar years. Views that fall under this analysis tend to see the reign of Christ as occurring through the ministry of the church during the church age, in which we currently live. Jesus's second coming, the resurrection, the judgment, and the eternal states will follow this current age.

Theologian James Leo Garrett provides helpful comparison of these views. Premillennialists and postmillennialists generally agree on a literal, 1,000-year transitional period between history and eternity, but they do not agree on the nature of that reign or its relation to Christ's return. Postmillennialists and amillennialists agree that Jesus's second coming will bring about the end of human history and be followed by one resurrection and one judgment, but they disagree on whether the millennium is literal or not. Premillennialists and amillennialists agree that the second coming of Christ could occur at any moment, but they do not agree on whether the millennium is literal, whether to expect multiple resurrections and judgments, and whether the millennium will be Jewish or Christian in character.[2]

In recent years, premillennialism has been the most prominent view among evangelicals, and two other concepts within that framework merit mentioning here: tribulation and rapture.

The tribulation refers to intense trials that will come near the end of all things. The New Testament refers to these at various points, including Matthew 24 and Revelation 2 and 7. Within a premillennialist framework, these tribulations are expected before Christ's 1,000-year rule. However, the relationship of the tribulation to the next term, rapture, differs among premillennialists.

The rapture refers to a concept that Paul teaches in 1 Thess 4:17. There, he wrote of the return of Christ and believers—those living and those who

---

[2] James Leo Garrett Jr., *Systematic Theology*, vol. 2 (Eugene, OR: Wipf & Stock, 2014), 750.

have died—meeting Christ "in the air." In the premillennial framework, this would occur before Christ's reign, but Christians disagree on its relationship to the tribulation. Some believe that Christ will rapture believers away from the earth before the period of the tribulation, so that they do not experience it and instead return triumphantly with Christ at the end of the tribulation (this position is referred to as pre-tribulational rapture, for obvious reasons). Others believe that Christ will instead sustain his people on earth during this time of trials, and they will be raptured at the end of the tribulation period, immediately before the beginning of the 1,000-year reign. (This position is referred to as *post-tribulational rapture*).

It is beyond the scope of this book to adjudicate these differences, but it is important to understand these different interpretations, and the different interpretations of the millennium, for a few reasons. First, these eschatological positions impact the way believers consider the role of the church in the current age, especially with reference to earthly governments. Postmillennialism in particular holds out great hope for conversion, righteousness, and godly government before the return of Christ. Second, these positions impact how Christians think about trials and tribulations that they might experience on earth. Third, these positions remind us that although Scripture is less clear on the exact details of what Christ's return will look like, the promise of his return is meant to provide encouragement and hope amid whatever we face.

Next, the doctrine of last things includes the doctrine of the resurrection. Both the Old Testament and the New Testament anticipate resurrection (e.g., see Isaiah 26, Mark 12, and John 5). Paul wrote about it in 1 Corinthians 15, teaching believers that those who have died will be raised and transformed. This transformation not only connects to the final hope of glorification that we introduced when discussing salvation; it also refers to the fact that we will have resurrection bodies like Jesus's. In the resurrection accounts in the Gospels, a few things become clear about these resurrection bodies. First, they are physical. Jesus told Thomas to touch him. Jesus ate after his resurrection. Second, they bear resemblance to our earthly bodies. The disciples recognized Jesus (except for those traveling with him at night on the road to Emmaus, but something entirely different was at work there than mere physical recognition). When Thomas saw Jesus, he even saw the marks of his wounds. But third, these bodies are not identical to our previous bodies. The Gospels tell us that Jesus appeared in rooms and the disciples were not exactly sure how he got in.

Therefore, while we should expect considerable continuity between our earthly bodies and our resurrection bodies, the resurrection body is a perfected body that will be different in ways we cannot yet understand or anticipate.

The doctrine of the resurrection does not only apply to those who are in Christ. Scripture teaches that the unrighteous are raised as well. Unbelievers are raised to undergo the final judgment, which we will deal with next.

The final judgment is a future event when the deeds done in the body are made known and judged by Christ. According to Scripture, this occurs after the millennial reign and serves as the transition point into eternity. The Bible clearly teaches this judgment. In Matthew 25, we see Jesus as judge. There, in 2 Corinthians 5 and in Hebrews 9, it is clear that all humans will be judged. In Romans 10, Paul emphasizes that all will stand before the judgment seat of God, being judged based on their earthly lives. In 2 Corinthians 5, we clearly see this judgment is permanent and final. For unbelievers, the final judgment should bring fear and encourage trust in Christ. (While many are rightly critical of "fire and brimstone" preachers who try to scare people, many Christians have gone so far in the opposite direction that they act like punishment isn't real or should not be feared. It is real. It should be feared. And such fear should be one factor motivating trust in Christ.) For believers, final judgment should not bring fear but assurance, because God has promised that we will be measured according to the merits of Christ, as we learned with the doctrine of justification. Some Christians believe that the sins of the righteous will indeed be revealed and judged at the final judgment, but they will be revealed as forgiven to glorify the Savior. In either case, the right response of believers is not fear but faith and gratitude.

Believers and unbelievers are not raised only to experience this judgment, but to exist eternally based on the results of this judgment. Theologians sometimes refer to these different outcomes as "eternal states." Two features to highlight here: First, these eternal states of blessing and punishment are different from the intermediate state, as discussed above. Second, these eternal states are eternal. This point is more controversial, but Christ himself teaches it in Matthew 25: the righteous go away into eternal life, and the unrighteous into eternal punishment.

Throughout the Bible, the most severe language is reserved for the punishment of those who have rebelled against God. Whether it is in places like Matthew 25, which we've just seen, or in parables such as the Wedding Banquet, with those outside being described as weeping and gnashing their teeth (Matt 8:12), harsh language is used. The picture in Scripture is eternal suffering, intense anguish, and loneliness. The wicked will recognize that God is who he has revealed himself to be in the final judgment, and then they will be separated from him and from his glory. We see that every knee will bow and every tongue confess that Jesus Christ is Lord (Phil 2:10–11). That includes the righteous and the unrighteous. That doesn't mean the unrighteous get one more chance; it means that they are lost, and they know it. Some theologians have dug into this language and proposed different conclusions. For instance, some note that the word used in the New Testament for this punishment was also used for a garbage dump outside Jerusalem. One way of reading that connection is to emphasize that garbage is burned and ceases to exist, so we should read the "eternal punishment" of the wicked as ceasing to exist, not being punished forever. (This position is called *annihilationism*). However, this conclusion does not automatically follow from the usage of the word. It still stands that the New Testament authors are using the harshest language they can find to describe this judgment. Fire, for them, would not necessarily have indicated annihilation, but continued anguish and pain. The problem with this is that words like everlasting, eternal and forever are used to refer to the wicked. There's eternal fire in Matthew 18, eternal contempt in Daniel 12, and eternal destruction in 2 Thessalonians. The emphasis is on how terrible this punishment will be, not so that people will lighten it through interpretation ("It surely can't mean *eternal* punishment"), but instead to drive them to the foot of the cross and recognition of their Savior and only hope.

The eternal states of those who have trusted Christ are provided in a very different picture, but still one that is difficult to wrap our minds around. Just as the language for the punishment is meant to emphasize its severity, the language for eternal life is meant to make clear how far above our imaginations the blessing and joy will be. In 1 Corinthians 13, Paul reminds us that we see a dim and distorted reality right now, but one day we will fully understand. We can only understand the blessing that we're promised in a partial and dim way now. However, a few points are revealed. First, we see that God will remove evils and pain (1 Cor 13:11–13). Second, we know that eternal life will be in a place of great glory (Revelation 21). Revelation's description of the New Jerusalem—pure gold, jewels—is using the most exalted language to describe this future reality. Third, eternal life is not marked by frenzied work but deep and full rest in the work of Christ, a rest connected to the rest that God entered on the seventh day of creation (Heb 4:1–11).

CONCLUSION

When it comes to the doctrine of last things, we are in territory where Christians disagree, or, to put it another way, find different and compelling ways of putting the various texts from Scripture together to help shape our expectations. Doctrines such as this remind me of one of my favorite Bible verses, Deut 29:29 (ESV), which begins with "The secret things belong to the LORD our God." Indeed, they do. And he has revealed some of those things, but not all of them.

As we finish this doctrine, remember the point with which we started this chapter: eschatology is meant to be a source of hope for the Christian life. These great truths, these hidden secrets, are meant not to strike fear in the heart of the believer but hope, encouragement, and certainty. Whatever things might look like in the world around us, God is in the process of fulfilling all his promises, all of the promises that ultimately find their "Yes" in Jesus Christ (2 Cor 1:20).

Engineering and the Doctrine of Eschatology
JEANNETTE RUSS

Are there assumptions or goals that are common in engineering that relate to making the world a better place or fixing major problems? And can you give some examples?

Many people define engineering as a problem-solving discipline. While I would argue that there are better definitions, it is certainly true that engineers generally have the mindset that problems can be solved: we have the tools, we have the abilities, and we have the training to solve or at least mitigate many problems. Examples abound, including:

- image-guided surgery in health care
- machines and public services in transportation

- alternative energy sources and more efficient use of traditional energy sources in power generation, storage, and delivery
- farm equipment and resource optimization in food production
- clean water and other services in public utilities

Some of these examples have a natural connection to missions, which we regularly discuss with students in our department. Missions often requires bridging a gap. Some communities are not interested in listening to traditional missionaries, but if a missionary can bring them something they want or need, such as solar-powered lighting or clean water, they can typically gain a hearing for sharing the gospel.

How does the Christian faith encourage engineers toward excellence in their work?

The Christian faith aligns very nicely with the professional code of ethics in engineering, which emphasizes safety, competence, transparency, and honesty (among other things). Because engineering is a profession that, in many cases, directly affects the public, most engineers are careful to do honest, ethical, and even excellent work. In that sense, there is very little difference between a Christian engineer and a non-Christian engineer.

However, the Christian faith could give engineers more of an internal motivation to strive for excellence. Like Christians in all disciplines, we should approach our work with diligence, joy, and love for others. One of the core values of Union University is "people-focused," and we often remind our students that the *things* we design or the *projects* we complete are ultimately for *people*—and so our focus should always be on the end user. I believe this intentional user-focused mentality drives the Christian engineer to pursue excellence in the sense of being open to what people want or need, being humble enough to listen to input, and being careful to address the problem at hand.

What do Christian engineers see about the world that other believers might miss or misunderstand?

First, we see order. We see order everywhere, and we like order! Our world has a tremendous amount of order, and the physical order of our universe is essential to sustain human life. A physicist spoke in chapel some years ago and referred to "the blessings of a boring universe." I love that phrase! In some sense, of course, the universe is anything but boring. However, there is an overall rhythm—an order—that we depend upon whether we realize it or not. Every day has twenty-four hours; the tides ebb and flow; the moon waxes and wanes. These elements of our universe are dictated by order, and they bless us.

Second, I think engineers can often see both sides of an issue and inherently seek to balance those opposing sides. For example, consider the ideal gas law: $PV = nRT$. You must balance pressure and volume to maintain the same value, so a tradeoff must be made. Is it preferable to have more pressure and less volume, or more volume and less pressure? You cannot increase both simultaneously without also changing either the amount of the gas (n) or the temperature (T). (R is the ideal gas constant and will not change.) While this example is a simple one, I believe that the ability to seek balance and understand tradeoffs can help engineers—or anyone trained in the STEM disciplines—have a clearer view of complex systems in society as well as scientific systems. In political systems, economic systems, and other complex social systems, the ability to see an issue from several points of view is an invaluable skill, especially when combined with an understanding that changing one variable will affect an entire system. An engineer who ponders these broader societal issues often seeks balance and understands that one must carefully attempt to anticipate the possible consequences of changing any variable, however small, in a complex system.

Third, engineers tend to see organized systems as a helpful approach to productivity. For example, when writing computer code, we generally reuse pieces of code that do common tasks such as memory allocation. We do not write new code line by line every time we start a new program, because we can so easily build upon selected pieces to accomplish subtasks, saving time and effort. Systematic organization is wonderful and applies to so many things in life. I will wade into some controversial waters here by commenting on evolution: Consider the biological system of lungs and consider further that many mammals have similar lung patterns. Does this similarity mean that mammalian lungs all evolved from a common ancestor, or is it possible that the Lord created a mammalian lung and decided he had made a good thing that he could reuse? I would humbly suggest that if humans are smart enough to reuse systems and subsystems, we might have inherited that idea from the Great Designer who graciously formed us in his image.

When is it hard to be a Christian engineer? For instance, do you think some engineers are set on fixing problems as though we can fix all problems on our own? Or put another way, does engineering tempt Christians toward a utopia that we know only Christ can bring?

Most of the engineers I know do not have any illusions about our ability to usher in societal utopia. Engineers tend toward worst-case scenarios in the sense of recognizing that if anything can possibly go wrong with technology, it probably will at some point. Designing for both expected and unexpected consequences is an often-discussed need in engineering circles, which keeps us humble enough to generally realize that we are not heading toward utopia on our own strength.

On the other hand, there are certainly some engineers who believe in a tech-based utopia, and I suppose there could be some unscrupulous engineers who might try to manipulate people into believing that utopia can be achieved through technology. However, I do not personally know any engineers in either of those categories. Christian engineers would, in most cases, be very aware of our human limitations and would consequently be able to differentiate between the hope we place in technology (and it does provide hope) and the infinitely greater hope we place in Almighty God.

How does engineering contribute to the kingdom of God? Are there pitfalls to avoid?

Engineers are creators by nature! We want to design interesting items and share them with the world, which I see as a contribution to God's kingdom. I also believe a focus on creation helps us understand one small aspect of being made in the image of God—the ultimate Creator. Christian engineers tend to realize that our Lord contributes to our ability to create by giving us so many models. Biomimicry is a big concept in robotics these days among both Christian and secular engineers, and it is certainly true that many aspects of design from the animal kingdom have led to advances in robotics. Christian engineers recognize that we are secondary creators: We do not create our own materials, and we sometimes do not even create our own ideas. So, to summarize, one contribution we make to God's kingdom is creativity, but we do so with humility by acknowledging that God is the ultimate Creator.

As a specific example of creativity, engineers are involved in producing items used in both warfare and farming, two very different pursuits. Consider the biblical references to beating "swords into plowshares" from Isa 2:4 (ESV) and "plowshares into swords" from Joel 3:10 (ESV). I like to think that engineers will be involved in the millennial transition from constant warfare to the reign of the Prince of Peace by finding creative ways to engineer instruments of war into items that are useful during times of great peace. Precedent has already been set for such activity, since many war-time technological advances have later been repurposed to contribute more broadly to society.

Regarding pitfalls, I think some engineers struggle with pride, since people tend to associate engineering with a certain level of intellectual ability. On the other hand, engineers are also often associated with introversion or even beyond introversion to a certain degree of social awkwardness, so perhaps that stereotype helps to mitigate any pride! Seriously, there are so many pitfalls to avoid with just being a sinner that it is difficult for me to determine which pitfalls are specifically related to engineering. I love being an engineer, but I love it even more when I view my profession through the lens of what it takes to walk with the Lord, attempting to follow his plan for my life in all areas. That final thought is the same for all professions, which is as it should be: the Lord calls us to different things, and we should do whatever he calls us to do with excellence and with a goal to glorify him.

Related Scripture

Isaiah 65:17–25
Isaiah 66:15–24
Matthew 25:31–46
John 5:24
John 6:40
Acts 1:9–11

1 Thessalonians 4:15–17
Revelation 21:1–8

FURTHER READING

Blomberg, Craig L., and Sung Wook Chung, eds. *A Case for Historic Premillennialism: An Alternative to "Left Behind" Eschatology.* Grand Rapids: Baker Academic, 2009.

Bock, Darrell L., ed. *Three Views on the Millennium and Beyond.* Grand Rapids: Zondervan, 1999.

Clouse, Robert. *The Meaning of the Millennium: Four Views.* Downers Grove, IL: IVP, 1977.

Erickson, Millard. *A Basic Guide to Eschatology.* Grand Rapids: Baker, 1998.

Höhne, David. *The Last Things.* Downers Grove, IL: IVP, 2019.

Middleton, J. Richard. *A New Heaven and a New Earth: Reclaiming Biblical Eschatology.* Grand Rapids: Baker Academic, 2014.

Conclusion

W hen I teach Christian Doctrine, I always include a basic statement on the first day and again toward the end of the semester. "I do not intend to answer every single question that you have about Christian Doctrine in this class. I hope we will answer some, but I also hope that you will leave the class with more questions than you started with. And hopefully better, more interesting questions." The same is true for this book. This is a *short* introduction to an infinitely vast field because God is not a limited creature like we are, or like any other field of study (eventually) is: finite. I hope you leave this book with more questions; I hope you leave somewhat unsatisfied, because you recognize a hunger within yourself to know God more fully.

At the same time, I try to protect students from short-circuiting the life of faith. Just because we acknowledge that we will never answer every question we have about theology, it does not follow that we should stop asking the questions or be satisfied with simple answers. I also remind students that, contrary to popular belief, we do not encourage more questions simply because what really matters is the questions, not the answers (or, similarly, that "life is about the journey, not the destination"). No, the answers do indeed matter. The knowledge of God for the sake of loving and serving God is what we are after, and God promises to reveal himself to those who seek him and his ways (Prov 3:6, for instance). I hope that this book has helped you answer some questions, but also helped you raise others, questions that might animate your faithful seeking of God's face, even as you also seek the knowledge and wisdom of your academic discipline. Questions that might lead you into some of the verses and books at the end of each chapter, even!

As you close this book on doctrines and Christian education, I pray that God will use it in a small way to continue to sharpen you and use you in the lives of your students. They will "read" your class sessions—and your lives—more carefully than most books!

Contributors

Haelim Allen is associate professor of art at Union University.

Sarah Bracey is assistant professor of psychology at Welch College.

Aaron Brown is assistant professor of English at LeTourneau University.

Matt Henderson is associate professor of sociology at Union University.

Greg Jordan is professor of law and ethics at Union University.

Rick Martinez is distinguished professor of management at North Greenville University.

Blake McKinney is assistant professor of history and humanities at Texas Baptist College.

Ross Parker is associate professor of Christian studies at Charleston Southern University.

Anna Rose Robertson is instructor of exercise science at Welch College.

Jeannette Russ is professor of engineering at Union University.

Micah Watson is associate professor in the department of politics and economics at Calvin University.

Jill Wells is assistant professor of social work at Union University.

Acknowledgments

As I finish this work and re-read the kind foreword by Dr. Dockery, I am reminded of something he frequently told us during his presidency at Union: as Christian scholars and Christian students, we stand on the shoulders of giants. He surely is one in the world of Christian higher education, and I am blessed to have been a beneficiary of his leadership, his scholarship, his kindness, and a presidential scholarship that made a Christian education possible for this first-generation college student.

My formal education was facilitated by many incredible thinkers and teachers. Brad Green, Greg Thornbury, Gary Smith, Mark Dubis, and Gene Fant (at Union), Jonathan Pennington and Al Mohler (at Southern Seminary), and Ralph Del Colle and Steve Long (at Marquette University) shaped me in ways I am only continuing to discover.

I have learned to teach and thrive within Christian academia with wonderful colleagues. Specifically, Roy Millhouse, Tom Bronleewe, Jeff Darnauer, Jenny Bradley, and Tim Gabrielson at Sterling College, Nathan Lane, Justin Hardin, Karelynne Ayayo, and Kathy Maxwell at Palm Beach Atlantic University, and all my School of Theology & Missions colleagues here at Union, under the leadership of our excellent dean, Ray Van Neste. Colleagues who have since moved elsewhere continue to be friends and sounding boards: C. Ben Mitchell and Nathan Finn, in particular, encouraged this specific project.

Union has provided so many colleagues across the university to teach, write, discuss, and grow with. Nan Thomas and Ann Singleton have made me a much better teacher and faculty member through their patient work. Phil Davignon, Joy Moore, Jay Beavers, and Jason Crawford put up with me in a writing group for several semesters before the pandemic upended so many of our rituals.

I have also had the privilege of flourishing and growing under the godly, brave, and mission-driven leadership of my provost John Netland and president Dub Oliver.

I am thankful to the gifted contributors who agreed to help me flesh out what this vision for "faithful learning" might look like in specific disciplines. Some are current or former colleagues, others former classmates, others I've not even met, but they were recommended to me and were kind enough to give this a whirl. (One was even briefly my landlord.) The book is much better because of their efforts. Thanks also to Julie Chhim, Claire White, and Leah Sutton for editorial help in various capacities, and to Mike Garrett for aid in compiling additional resources for each chapter.

Finally, my wife, Keshia, and our children, Ezekiel, Jackson, Ramona, and Lena, continue to love and encourage me. They are a daily reminder of the true gift that family is—whether they eat their dinner or not. As the kids grow, my hope and prayer are that they will end up in the classrooms and offices of the kind of faculty that this book is aimed at.

Name and Subject Index